I'd Rather We Got Casinos

I'd Rather We Got Casinos

and OTHER BLACK THOUGHTS

Larry Wilmore

HYPERION

NEW YORK

Library of Congress Cataloging-in-Publication Data

Wilmore, Larry.
    I'd rather we got casinos, and other Black
thoughts / Larry Wilmore.
        p.   cm.
    ISBN 978-1-4013-0955-8
    1. United States—Race relations.   2. African
Americans—Race identity.   3. Racism—United
States.   I. Title.
    E185.615.W535   2008
    305.800973—dc22

                                    2008026526

Hyperion books are available for special
promotions, premiums, or corporate training.
For details contact Michael Rentas, Proprietary
Markets, Hyperion, 77 West 66th Street,
12th floor, New York, New York 10023, or call
212-456-0133.

FIRST EDITION

10   9   8   7   6   5   4   3   2   1

I would like to dedicate this book
to my nephew, Timmy,
whose laugh will never be forgotten.

CONTENTS

ACKNOWLEDGMENTS

I would like to first thank my wife, Leilani, for all her support and encouragement. I couldn't have done it without her.

Thanks to my children, John and Lauren, for always rooting me on and making me laugh.

Thanks to my parents, Betty and Larry, for being funny and not knowing it.

Thanks to my siblings, Juanita, Debbie, Marc, Brenda, and David, for being funny and knowing it.

Thanks to Anto, Wellington, Dan, Don, Nelson, Tip, Parsa, Arbi, Kev, Tom, Paul, and everyone else at the cigar shop for constantly uttering the phrase, "Hey man, you done with that book yet?"

Thanks to Jon Stewart and everyone at *The Daily*

Acknowledgments

Show for their support and feeling my "I can't believe I agreed to write this @%&* book" pain.

Thanks to Cheryl Dolins for laughing at this idea first.

Thanks to Daniel Greenberg for making all of this happen.

Thanks to Will Schwalbe for taking a chance on a first book, and for those awesome cupcakes.

Thanks to Gretchen Young for her incredible patience and generosity, particularly through the difficult time I had writing after the death of my nephew. Her kindness and understanding during my tardiness will always be appreciated.

Thanks to everyone at Hyperion for all of their hard work and support.

Thanks to Michael Rotenberg and David Miner for their guidance and vision.

A special thanks to Vicki Tunstall and Marc Wax for believing in me years ago before anyone else did.

A very special thanks to Tom Hoberman for all of his wisdom, expertise, and friendship. Your professional and personal support are without equal.

INTRODUCTION

I am extremely jealous of you right now. I have spent the last decade and a half clipping newspaper articles, taping television programs, transcribing radio interviews, and showing up uninvited to personal appearances of a man whose "black thoughts" have changed my life. I have begged, pleaded, and bribed this same man to allow me to present these to the world. He finally relented and you get to drink it all up in one serving.

I first became familiar with Mr. Wilmore and his particular insights into the culture at large from a black perspective or, as I said earlier, his "black thoughts," shortly after the Rodney King beating. He was being interviewed on a radio program and the subject of black history month came up. They were discussing its relevance, particularly in regard to better educating people on the unheralded accomplishments of many blacks in American society. When asked if he was in favor of it, he replied, "Hell, no."

When pushed to elaborate, Wilmore said, "Twenty-eight days of trivia to make up for centuries of oppression? I'd rather we got casinos!" Well, he had me at "Hell, no."

Since then, I've been a devout and devoted follower. It's hard to completely explain why, but I'll give it a shot. I believe it's his ability to find racism in almost any conceivable thing that intoxicates me the most.

For example, how many of you knew that "hope" was black? I thought it was insane at first myself until I heard Wilmore point out that if it weren't black, why would you need a "great white hope"? Not only does that make sense, it can be extrapolated even further.

The table was set for Barack Obama's historic run for the presidency by his book *The Audacity of Hope.* Now, if hope were not black, why would it need to be "audacious" to run for president? Wait, I'm not finished.

You may argue that President Clinton ran on the claim of being the "Man from Hope." What about that? Wilmore would argue back that he was also called "the first black president." And it wasn't for playing the sax and chasing chubby white girls.

You see what I mean? Only Wilmore could make that make sense. And by making that make sense, it actually *makes sense.*

Don't worry if you feel confused. Once you get through a couple of his essays, particularly his "Search for Black Jesus" and his call for television to "Bring Back the Shetland Negro," you'll be inebriated as well.

I've collected as many of Wilmore's "Black Thoughts" as I thought would give the best representation of his point of view. Some were never published and some are transcripts of radio shows and happenings. I've even included a few "Random Black Thoughts" that Wilmore had written down but hadn't yet developed.

So, I now present to you, *I'd Rather We Got Casinos, and Other Black Thoughts* by Larry Wilmore. I trust you'll enjoy it and remember, whenever you're hoping, you're having a black thought.

Professor Elister Morrison Lawrence
Director of the Historically Oppressed
Peoples Enterprise (H.O.P.E.)

I'd Rather We Got Casinos

A Time for Change

*W*ilmore contributed many pieces for the op-ed columns of major newspapers. One of my personal favorites was his proposed name change to help race relations. It's well thought through and one could argue it's full of merit. It actually received the most responses from readers of The Times of any column that month.

You always hear people say "racism is still a major part of everyday life." Most people accept this premise without investigating it further. Mainly because they agree with it and, secondly, they don't want to challenge it for fear of seeming like the racist in question. They also feel there's nothing they can do about it. It's racism, you can't change it. My problem with this statement is that it's too general. By using words like "racism" or "racists," it keeps the notion distant and "out there." It feels like a problem to be contemplated and discussed like a philosophical construct instead of a problem that could use a concrete solution like a backed-up sink.

If we imagine racism as a backed-up sink, the solution becomes clearer. Unclog it. Look into the drain, see what's backing it up, and get that crap out of there. Now, the more practical question: How is this accomplished? How do we get people of different colors to learn to live in harmony? People smarter than me have struggled for eons twisting the sides of this societal Rubik's Cube while secretly fearing there is no real solution. I believe the answer lies in asking the right question. We should not ask, "How do we get rid of racism?" Our question should be "How do we turn racism into a sink?" We could start with a name change.

I know "a rose by any other name would smell as sweet," to quote Shakespeare. But keep in mind, we're not trying to get rid of the smell of racism. That stink will probably be around forever. We're trying to ease the pain of it and clear the way for us to get along peacefully. That's right, we're unclogging the sink.

Before I propose the name changes, let's first examine whether or not name change is effective. I would argue it is not only effective but essential to success in many cases. Take actors for example. Do you think red-necks would ever line up to see a movie starring a rugged all-American cowboy named Marion Morrison? Of course not. But if his name is John Wayne, the line is around the block and into the next county. Everybody loved Lucy but do you think we would have even liked Dianne Désirée Belmont? Nobody would've given a flying f@*k. Back in the Twenties, MGM actually had a contest for people to come up with a name for their budding starlet Lucille Fay Le Sueur. The winning name was Joan Crawford. It's unsure America would've cozied up to father figure Alphonso D'Abruzzo to comfort them during the cynical seventies. But Alan Alda filled the bill perfectly. Sometimes the changes aren't that big but still significant. Ving Rhames's real name is Irving Rhames. Ving was smart enough to realize that when you think about it, no brother should really ever be called Irving.

And it's not just actors. Companies for years have realized the power of name changing. Branding, as they call it. I can't imagine anyone wanting to BackRub the Internet for information. But we love to Google. You'll never catch me fiddling with my Marafuku but I can't put down my Nintendo. And what science fiction movie did you walk into to buy that Radar Range? I'll stick with my microwave, thank you very much. You see where I'm going? You can't change the face of racism without changing the name. Change the way people feel about it. Brand it. You may be asking, "But Larry, why would we want to soften such a hateful word? Don't we want people to take it seriously?" Yes. That's why I propose we leave the word "racism" alone. I suggest we change the term "African-American."

African-American, as a brand, is done. It's served its purpose. It did what it was supposed to do. But now, it's time for it to step aside. It's so twentieth century anyway. First of all, no one really wants to be called African-American anymore. You see, as a black, this politically correct term doesn't conjure up images of the struggle my people have faced in this country for several hundred years. When I hear African-American, my mind doesn't snap back to the march on Selma or the bus boycotts. It doesn't stir up nostalgia for Joe Louis or the Harlem Renaissance. I'm not charged with pride by our victory over slavery or Tiger's at the Masters. It doesn't even make my stomach growl for hog maws or black-eyed peas. It just makes me think of Africa. And to be blunt, I'm not that crazy about Africa.

I mean, I know that's where we come from, it's our heritage, and blah, blah, blah. "Africa" just makes me think of hot. A hot land where you have to hunt your food, black people speak French, and you might get malaria.

I'm sorry but that's just not very sexy. And if I want to be around black people who talk different in an unbearably hot environment where my ancestors once roamed, I'll go to the check-cashing place.

And for the nonblacks who have to remember to use it, lest they be called racist, it's frankly become a mouthful. It wears them down to constantly say "black—oops, sorry, African-American, bla—oops sorry, African-American, ni—oops sorry, African-American" (just kidding). Let's be honest, whites have a tremendous amount of collective guilt about slavery. And the word "African" just reminds them of it. Don't get me wrong. There was a time when it was proper to shove this down their throats. But now they have a gag reflex and that doesn't help anyone.

You could argue it doesn't matter what we call ourselves or what people call us, there's always going to be a reminder of the past. Not necessarily. We were very close to making a breakthrough in the seventies when we had people call us Afro-Americans. That was an effing awesome name. It didn't remind anyone of Africa or slavery and it was fun. I mean, who doesn't love an Afro?

My proposal is to put fun back in our name, shake off the past, and barrel toward the future. A name that plants us firmly in the twenty-first century and beyond. It'd be nice to return to Afro-American but we used black right after that and unfortunately the "once you go black" rule applies. But that's okay, we're a very creative bunch and I know someone will think of something great.

The important thing to remember is that it has to make sense. You can't just pick something random like "boomerang." Yeah, it makes me think of the Eddie Murphy movie but I also think of Australia, so, not good. A great pitch would be "chocolate." Once again, who doesn't love chocolate? It's a fun name, it's easily modified, and instead of slavery, it makes people think of dessert.

Chocolate is a great way to wean people off of not just African-American but all of the variations of designation society has confected. No more black, negro, colored, mulatto, high yellow, passing, mixed, French, half-breed, halfrican-American, Indian in me, or cablinasian (Caucasian, black, Indian, and Asian—this is how Tiger Woods once described himself). We're all just different types of chocolate.

This also makes traveling abroad much easier. If you see a brother in London, you don't want to be stuck trying to figure out, Is he African-American, no this is England; African-English, no that doesn't sound right. He's chocolate! Done. Enjoy the rest of your vacation. "But what if I see a dark Middle Easterner? What do I call him?" Don't call him anything. Just let it go. One sink at a time, my brotha, one sink at a time.

Take Me to Your Leader

*W*ilmore always felt it was unfair that most so-called black leaders were self-appointed. He wondered why there was never an election. Why don't black people get a chance to vote for the person they want to be their leader? In the following speech, Wilmore makes the case that that leader should be him.

My fellow African-Americans, black people, people of color, colored people, Negroes, I come before you today as a humble servant in the struggle for equality and justice. This struggle has taken us from slave ships to sitcoms. From antebellum to Aunt Jemima. From Jim Crow to O.J. From white to white privilege to black-on-black crime.

No part of this struggle has been without pain. No part of this struggle has been without sacrifice. And no part of this struggle has been without hope. I'm here to continue that hope. I'm here to help end that struggle. I'm here to help point the way to a new direction for our people. I'm here to be your black leader.

Many of you may ask, Why? Why do we need a black leader? Or, more specifically, why do black people need a leader? My answer to that is, Who cares? We blacks just like having leaders and I want to be the next one. What are my qualifications? I'm black and I want the job. Nuff said. Now, I know that's not going to satisfy the small minority of people who need a little more. No problem. I can do that. Just keep in mind most black leaders are self-appointed and at any time I can play that card and end the whole discussion. Okay, here it goes:

I'M REALLY GOOD AT RHYMING.

This may sound like nothing on the surface but if you dig down deep enough you'll see that you can take any issue and make it seem more important by rhyming. Case in point, taxes. At first glance it would seem like it would be difficult to make taxes an important issue for blacks, let alone make white people feel like they're being racist, which when push comes to shove should always be the goal. For instance, if I said, "We need to ease the tax burden on the poor and middle class to help raise their standard of living," you would probably say, "No thanks, so-called black leader."

But if I said, "First it was guns and axes, now they wanna kill us with taxes," you would probably say, "Preach it, black leader." Or how about, "They minimize peace and max out hate, now they wanna lower the top tax rate?" Tell me that doesn't make you want to light a dirty T-shirt to burn down your neighborhood?

And that's just taxes; I can effectively rhyme any issue from abortion to school vouchers. What other black leader would even think of rhyming vouchers? For this reason alone I should be your black leader. But don't worry, I have more.

I CAN FIND BLAME IN PLACES YOU HAVEN'T EVEN THOUGHT OF LOOKING YET.

To be an effective black leader, one must be able to blame the Man for just about everything. The problem is, most black leaders are ambulance chasers. That is to say, they follow the tragedy of the day instead of doing the hard work and finding blame in the cracks and crevices of society. I don't need a crisis at the Louvre to get me to start looking for the Da Vinci code. If you tell me the Man had a hand in something, no matter what it is, I'm telling you that hand's got some black on it. Even if I have to make it up first and prove it later, I'll find it. And even if I don't prove it later, too bad. I've effectively played the race card and have moved on to another issue.

For example, school lunches are racist. You're saying, "What do you mean, school lunches are racist? Where is the proof of that?" It doesn't matter. By the time we get to the point where I actually have to provide some solid examples to back up my claim, everyone has accepted that there's probably some racism in school lunches somewhere. And if you resist too much, you're probably a racist for not believing me. My point being, who would've thought to look for racism in school lunches? Your next self-appointed black leader would.

YOU'LL NEVER BE ABLE TO PIN DOWN WHAT I DO FOR A LIVING.

All good black leaders have mysterious jobs and I am no exception. I get paid, but by whom? I go to work every morning, but to where? I do what I do because I'm very good at it. Yeah, but what is that? These and more frustrating questions will enter the minds of many of my critics, who will try to use my profession as a wedge issue. Good luck. They can't use what they can't find.

The most I'll ever give anybody is a hint of an occupation that seems somewhat linked to whatever issue I'm protesting. I call this the "moving target résumé." For instance, if I'm leading a march on racial harassment in factories, I can make vague allusions to the time I worked in a factory and conditions were even worse. If someone presses me to be more specific, I'll just call him a racist for questioning my past and move on.

White people will be so confused trying to figure out what I do or did for a living that the confusing rhetoric I'll use to get my point across will sail right past them. I can't stress enough the importance of distracting white people when you're arguing about race. It really throws them off their game.

I'M A REVEREND WITH NO CHURCH.

In order to be an effective black leader you have to have "reverend" in your name. It gives you instant gravitas in the black community and prevents people from attacking you too harshly. After all, an attack on me is an attack on Jesus. It's not true, but who cares? I said it and that's good enough to stop the discussion.

Also, I get to speak really loud and everybody thinks it's normal. Most human beings don't shout during normal conversations. But with "reverend" in my name, I can shout no matter what the topic. Think of how versatile this can be. The subject might be Jell-O, everybody's calm, and then bam, I'm shouting. What the fuck? Relax, I'm a reverend, I can shout at anything. Remember, it's very important for your black leader to be able to raise his voice without getting angry. Anger is a tool to be used sparingly. Shouting sounds like anger and has similar effects, but you can always shrug it off as your style.

WHEN I GET ANGRY, WHITE PEOPLE ARE AFRAID OF ME.

Anger is one of the most effective tools a black leader can use against the establishment, and I promise to have it in spades. Unlike shouting, anger is a seldom-to-be-used tactic to firmly draw the line and send the signal that you're tired of someone's racist behavior and the conversation can't continue until they stop being racist.

Also, my anger isn't loud and garrulous like most black leaders. It's brooding and hurt. I don't want white people to think they made me mad, I want them to think they hurt me: "I thought our relationship was great and then they do this." They will want to do all they can to repair the relationship; they can't help it.

I LOVE CAMERA TIME.

It's extremely vital that your black leader be on TV as much as possible. Good news: I am a camera whore. I cannot get enough of my face being drawn out by millions of electrons racing across a plasma screen. It's my crack, I admit it. And like crack, I'll do whatever it takes to get as much as I can.

Keep in mind, there doesn't have to be a civil rights issue on the table for me to get my face time. I can turn an appearance at a sporting event into a meaningful black leader sighting. Remember, the more people see me on TV, the more they accept me as the de facto black leader.

As you can see, I am completely prepared to be your black leader now. We live in a dangerous world and we need a black leader more than ever. As a race, we have a long way to go and I want to help get us to the finish line. But I can't do it without your help. Actually I can, because I'm appointing myself, but you know what I mean.

Man Talk

*W*ilmore, for a time, hosted a talk radio program. *Many of the transcripts have been lost but thankfully some of the most controversial ones have been preserved. One in particular, his conversation with the Man, was arguably the most intriguing. This took place about a month after Hurricane Katrina and the Man was taking quite a bit of heat for the way the government handled the disaster. The Man rarely sits down for interviews and so Wilmore really scored a coup by getting him on his program. We pick it up just after the first commercial break.*

WILMORE: That's where I bought my Lexus and you can too. Just ask for the friendly people at Circle Lexus. Tell them you heard this ad on *The Larry*

Wilmore Show. (Show music.) Welcome back, everyone. I'm Larry Wilmore and you're listening to *The Larry Wilmore Show.* Coming up in this hour I'll be speaking to the Man. I know many of you have been looking forward to this and frankly, so have I. He is definitely one of the hardest figures to pin down and I am honored that he would choose my show to discuss his role in the world and our lives, I guess you could say. He is joining us by phone. Would you please welcome to the show, the Man.

THE MAN: Hey, Larry. It's a pleasure to be on your show.

WILMORE: Hey, the Man, the pleasure's all mine. Thank you for taking the time out.

THE MAN: No problem. I'm a big fan. Long-time listener, first-time caller.

WILMORE: Ah, very funny. I'm sure you listen to my show.

THE MAN: Don't be so surprised. You know what they say about the Man, he's always listening.

WILMORE: You know, that is so true, I didn't even think about that. Since you put it out there, let's talk about that area of your mystique. Are you always listening?

THE MAN: Not always. I mean, I'm not Big Brother, I'm the Man. I have an idea of what's going on, most of the time, but I don't snoop. I only care about keeping the brothers down, I don't have an interest in their personal lives.

WILMORE: Oh, I see. So keeping a brother down is not a personal issue with you. You don't have a vendetta or agenda.

THE MAN: That's right, it's just a job, like fixing air conditioners. I just fix the system so you have a very difficult time getting over. But in the end, I put my pants on one leg at a time.

WILMORE: Interesting. You know most people think of the Man as some hulking oppressive bureaucratic monolith that lords over us from the shadows of the establishment. But you seem like a pretty normal cat.

THE MAN: Extremely normal. I watch *American Idol,* we just got a Wii, my kids are hitting puberty, the wife's on antidepressants, and I just wrapped up an m-f of a mid-life crisis.

WILMORE: Wait a second. The Man had a mid-life crisis?

THE MAN: Oh yeah. Young girlfriend, sports car, hip clothes, the whole works. I was such a pitiful cliché.

WILMORE: Unbelievable. I can't get over how human you are.

THE MAN: Thank you.

WILMORE: It's not a compliment. It's an observation. I mean, I've hated you all my life and it's very disarming to talk to you like you're one of the guys.

THE MAN: That's one of the reasons I wanted to do your show, Larry. To clear up some of the, uh, misconceptions and in some cases lies about who I am. I'm really looking forward to it.

WILMORE: As am I. I want to get to all of that and even take some calls, if that's okay with you?

THE MAN: Absolutely. The only thing I like better than talking to normal people is screwing them and getting in their way.

WILMORE: Beautiful. We'll continue our talk with the Man and take some of your calls right after this short break. (Show music.)

WILMORE: (Show music.) Welcome back to *The Larry Wilmore Show*. I'm your host, Larry Wilmore, and I am talking to controversial figure and father of two, the Man. Now, I have to ask, how do you get the job of the Man? Do you apply for it? Are you picked for it? Are you born into it? How does it work?

THE MAN: Great question, Larry. I can't really go into specifics, unfortunately, that's just the way it is. Let's just say it's not something that requires an application.

WILMORE: Fair enough. But it doesn't seem like it's something one would aspire to. You know what I mean? In other words, when an adult asks kids what they want to be when they grow up, no one says the Man.

THE MAN: True, but I believe a lot of that can be blamed on the liberal media. If kids knew how great a life they could have as the Man, you'd hear a lot more support from youngsters.

WILMORE: Of course, you just admitted to having a mid-life crisis.

THE MAN: Yes, but I did most of my healing from it at my vacation home in Tuscany.

WILMORE: Touché. Do you get enjoyment out of what you do? I mean, are screwing people and keeping brothers down fun?

THE MAN: Of course not. No one likes to see people hurt. I get my thrill out of the puzzle.

WILMORE: The puzzle?

THE MAN: Yes. The challenge of figuring out the right combination of events that conspire to possibly keep a brother down is what drives me. In other words, I don't like seeing a brother down, I just enjoy putting him there.

WILMORE: And the harder the puzzle, the bigger the thrill?

THE MAN: Exactly. If I see a brother who was raised in a nice middle-class family, great parents, loving mom and dad, never got in trouble, stayed away from drugs, and is well educated, I'm thinking good luck trying to find obstacles to put in his way.

WILMORE: In the puzzle analogy, that brother would be a sudoku?

THE MAN: Yes. Or the Sunday *New York Times* crossword. Tough but not impossible.

WILMORE: And finding those obstacles is what gives you joy?

THE MAN: Like a runner's high. He applies for a small business loan, I make sure it's denied because of some obscure zoning law, my endorphins release like crazy.

WILMORE: No doubt. Did that really happen?

THE MAN: I'm not at liberty to say.

WILMORE: Okay. So would it be fair to say that you are involved in a racial conspiracy?

THE MAN: No. Racial conspiracies are still handled by the government. You know Tuskegee, drug laws, Katrina—

WILMORE: Wait a second. You weren't responsible for Katrina? That wasn't the work of the Man?

THE MAN: Heavens no. Only the government could get away with that level of incompetence and cruelty. The Man focuses on the individual. I'm more of an annoying omnipresent speed bump, a reminder that you haven't yet arrived.

WILMORE: A thorn in your side. A pimp slap to your progress.

THE MAN: Exactly. I don't always win. Many people are able to get past me and have very successful and fulfilling lives.

WILMORE: They have to find a way to outsmart you. Figure out their own puzzle.

THE MAN: Precisely. It's like a game of chess. Move, countermove, move, countermove.

WILMORE: Or Whac-A-Mole. A brother sticks his head up and the Man whacks it back down. *Whack!*

THE MAN: That's right.

They both laugh.

THE MAN: That's great, you're going to have to let me borrow that.

WILMORE: You can borrow it, but I'm going to have to charge you a pretty high interest rate.

THE MAN: Ha! Very good. I guess you're the Man.

WILMORE: No, you da man!

They both laugh again.

WILMORE: Okay, that's fun. I have to say, I was so predisposed to not liking you but you are very charming.

THE MAN: Thank you. I return the compliment.

WILMORE: Thank you. Do you have time to take some calls?

THE MAN: Would love to.

WILMORE: Great. I tell you what. Let's take a quick break and go to some callers on the other side. Is that all right?

THE MAN: You da man.

WILMORE: Okay, enough of that. We'll be right back with your calls for the Man, right here on *The Larry Wilmore Show*. (Show music.)

WILMORE: (Show music.) Welcome back. You are listening to *The Larry Wilmore Show*. My guest today is the Man. A somewhat controversial figure in society.

THE MAN: I like to think of myself as misunderstood.

WILMORE: Misunderstood, fair enough. We are going to open up the lines for your calls. Okay, Darryl, you are on with Larry and the Man.

DARRYL: Hey, Larry, how're you doing today?

WILMORE: Not bad, thanks for asking.

DARRYL: No problem. Larry, I've been taught my whole life that your guest is responsible for a lot of the evils that exist in our society. My question is, how can he sleep with himself?

WILMORE: Darryl wants to know how can you sleep with yourself?

THE MAN: I use earplugs because I'm a horrible snorer. But seriously, I think, as I've stated before, that you have inflated the scope of deeds that I'm even capable of doing. I'm not saying you're doing it on purpose or blaming you. Once again, I blame the liberal media.

DARRYL: So, you weren't responsible for the Rodney King beating?

THE MAN: Good lord, no. That was a despicable, probably racist, act committed by rogue cops who were obviously out of control. Personally, I was disgusted by their behavior.

DARRYL: I'm glad to hear you say that. That was a dark chapter.

THE MAN: I agree.

DARRYL: And then the jury said they were not guilty.

THE MAN: Now that was me.

DARRYL: What? I thought you had nothing to do with it?

THE MAN: With the beating. That was heinous. But the acquittal's different. That fell more in the area of getting screwed by the system.

WILMORE: Screwed by the system. So the acquittal was directly aimed at Rodney King, to screw him, and not at black people in general?

THE MAN: Correct.

WILMORE: Does that make sense, Darryl?

DARRYL: Uh—

WILMORE: Good, let's go to our next caller. Debbie, you're on with Larry and the Man.

DEBBIE: Hi, Larry. Hi, the Man.

WILMORE: Hello.

THE MAN: Hi.

DEBBIE: Larry, first I want to say I'm a huge fan. I listen to you every day. You're the best.

WILMORE: Thank you.

DEBBIE: I've turned a lot of my friends on to you too. We never miss your happiness hour.

WILMORE: That's very nice of you. Do you have a question for the Man?

DEBBIE: Yes. How do you choose the people you're going to screw? I'll take the answer off the air.

WILMORE: All right. How does the selection process work?

THE MAN: That's a great question. Sometimes it's random. Uh, sometimes you'll get a last-minute notification that someone's got too much good stuff happening too often. Um, I might request one, though that's rare.

WILMORE: Really? Give me an example of someone you requested. You don't have to be specific, just give me the circumstances.

THE MAN: Sure. I noticed this gentleman, or brother, if you will, was applying for a mortgage to buy his dream home. He had saved years for the down payment and made a lot of sacrifices. It seemed to me he was just barely going to qualify so I felt something needed to be done.

WILMORE: You denied it?

THE MAN: No, I made sure it went through. He even got out of paying the closing costs.

WILMORE: Wow. I'm impressed. I didn't expect that from you.

THE MAN: Thank you.

WILMORE: I mean, that doesn't sound like something the Man would do. I would think you'd make sure he didn't get that loan.

THE MAN: It was a subprime. He lost the house six months later.

WILMORE: Damn, you really are good. Now, that's how the Man gets you! As soon as a brother can afford a house, his dream house no doubt, the Man finds a way to take it away. Brilliant.

THE MAN: Yeah, I was pretty proud of that.

WILMORE: I think we have time for one more. Can you stick around?

THE MAN: Let's do it.

WILMORE: Kevin, you're on with Larry and the Man.

KEVIN: The Maaaaaaaan. Heeeeeeey, how's it going?

THE MAN: Good.

KEVIN: You are awesome, man, awesome. You da maaaaaaaan.

THE MAN: Thank you.

WILMORE: We're almost out of time, what's your question?

KEVIN: Okay, uh, I was wondering, uh, okay, sorry, I'm a little nervous.

WILMORE: Just relax, he's not going to bite you.

KEVIN: Um, I just want to know, do you just screw with brothers?

WILMORE: Thank you, Kevin. Are brothers the only target?

THE MAN: In this country, yes. In Europe, it's the French.

WILMORE: All of the French people?

THE MAN: Oh, yeah. They were our first clients.

WILMORE: Will you be branching out?

THE MAN: We hope to. Right now, we're looking at
some of the first-generation immigrant groups in
this country, Asians, Mexicans, and some
Canadians.

WILMORE: Canadians? Really? Why Canadians?

THE MAN: I don't know, it just seems like screwing
them would just be a whole lot of fun and a great
challenge.

WILMORE: That's all our time for now. I want to thank
the Man for joining us this hour.

THE MAN: You're welcome, Larry. We'll have to smoke
a cigar sometime.

WILMORE: Absolutely. You can help me get rid of
some of those Cubans I've got stashed at the house.

THE MAN: You mean, the house the Customs officials
just seized?

WILMORE: Oh no, you didn't—

THE MAN: I'm just messing with you.

WILMORE: Whoa, you had me. I got scared for a second.

THE MAN: Or am I?

WILMORE: See, that's how the Man gets you. You get a little paranoid, then you drop your guard and then *bam*. You really are the Man. See ya around.

THE MAN: Yes you will.

WILMORE: Stay tuned for the next hour when we'll have open lines. Talk about anything you want. This is *The Larry Wilmore Show*. (Show music.)

A month after this interview, Wilmore was arrested for illegally purchasing Cuban cigars. The charges were eventually dropped on an obscure technicality. Wilmore never found out what that technicality was or who brought it up.

A Letter to the NAACP

*fter his op-ed asking for a name change from
African-American to chocolate, Wilmore decided to
take his case directly to the NAACP. This is the first of
several correspondences.*

Dear Sir,

First let me congratulate you on the wonderful
march and demonstration you conducted last
week. I saw it on TV and thought it was well
organized. I'm not sure what it was for but I know
it must've been something real racist. Bravo!

I'm writing you today about a pressing
concern of mine that I believe should be yours as
well. As you may or may not know, I make my

living as a cultural pundit. That is to say, people look to me for insights into the culture. In a recent editorial, I called upon our people to change our designation from African-American to chocolate. I won't bore you with the specifics (I've attached it as a pdf) except to try to convince you to climb aboard.

I know you guys are busy with all the race stuff and I know that's important. But I implore you to take the time to consider my argument. Chocolate really is the way to go. I've already tried it out on people and it's been an overwhelming success. At least four out of five black people like it and an impressive five out of five nonblacks do. In other words, everybody loves chocolate!

But I need your help. The NAACP has been the premier civil rights group of the last hundred years. Not only have you witnessed the untold number of horrible racial incidents during that period, you were there for all the previous name changes as well. From "colored" to "Negro" to "colored" again, to "the so-called negro" to "black" to "Afro-American," to "American of African descent" to "black" again, to "people of color" to "black" once more, and finally to "African-American." Through all of this, you have remained unchanged. You are still the National

Association for the Advancement of Colored People. In other words, you're not crazy about the term "African-American" either.

So get on the chocolate train!

Sorry for being so informal, but I can't mask my enthusiasm. As you'll read in the attached article, chocolate has so many advantages, including the best one: you don't have to change your initials! You can still be the NAACP. Only now it stands for the National Association for the Advancement of Chocolate People. Just think what this could do for fund-raising. Even the most dedicated bigot would want to send money to that group!

I really want you to think long and hard (that's what she said; sorry, I couldn't resist) about this before making your decision. If part of you feels this sounds like too silly a notion for an organization like the NAACP to embrace, consider this: after one of the most tragic natural disasters, followed by an equally tragic indifferent government response, Mayor Ray Nagin standing in the tortured remains of Hurricane Katrina said, "We have to rebuild Chocolate City."

Chocolate City!!

Now, you know and I know he was not referring to Hershey, Pennsylvania. He was talking about New Orleans and niggas! (Sorry for the "n" word, I got carried away again.) Keep in mind, no one blinked an eye when he said "chocolate." A few politically correct media people got their panties in a bunch but everybody else was cool.

All I'm saying is, let's continue what Mayor Nagin started. What better way to begin this new century than to honor the city that reminded us all that the struggle for equality continues?

Anyway, I won't take up any more of your time. I hope you see the potential and help me get this movement started. I'll be in touch and call me on my cell if you'd like to speak directly.

Thank you and take care.

Your "Milk Chocolate" Brotha,
Larry Wilmore
(cell 310-555-9889)
(chocolate5800612.pdf 135kb) attached

Black Weathermen Make Me Feel Happy

I'm not sure what periodical this was meant for but it was never published.

When I turn on the news, the lead story is always something tragic. Someone was raped, killed, or both. Something or someone blew up in the Middle East. People are starving somewhere far and near. Families are losing homes and homes are losing families. Stock prices go down as oil prices go up. There are pesticides in our foods, suicides in our schools, and genocides in Darfurs. The bad guys in the world have found another way to win and my home team has found another way to lose. It's not even fifteen past the hour and I feel so down that a double Red Bull with a selective serotonin reuptake inhibitor chaser couldn't rescue me from an imploding sense of ennui. Enter the black weatherman. Thank you, Jesus.

Black weathermen make me feel happy. I don't care how bad the story is before it gets "thrown" to them. They bring me joy. I don't know if they're doing it on purpose, if they're aware of it, or if it's just some divine gift they all share. All I know is, I can't get enough of them. And the fat ones make me feel happier than the skinny ones.

I'm not saying I laugh at their jokes or find their over-dependence on puns to be entertaining. I'm saying they make me feel happy. Like I said, especially the fat ones.

Do weathermen make me feel happy? Not necessarily. Do black newsmen make me feel happy? I don't think so. Do fat black people in general on TV make me feel happy? Not in any way I can measure. It's the intoxicating combination of black, weather, and fat that releases the endorphins locked in my brain. I like to call it the Roker Effect.

Al Roker has a gift. He was the first fat black weatherman—that I can recall—to lift my spirits. Though my mother recounts an incident that occurred during my toddler years when I always seemed to wet my diaper whenever they had the news on. It seems I was so happy, I peed my pants. Mom attributed the phenomenon to my love of television or even news. I felt it went deeper and after a little research was proven correct.

Apparently, back in the mid-sixties, our local TV station was one of the first to feature a fat black weatherman. His name was Big Johnny Page and he did the weather for the six o'clock news. I looked him up online and upon seeing his picture, immediately wet my pants.

Think about it. Even after more than forty years, the mere sight of this zoftig atmosphere prognosticator filled me with so much joy, my bladder had to empty to make room.

Anyway, back to the Roker Effect. I'm not alone, by the way. Many have reported a sense of joy when in the electronic presence of one of these superhumans, these sons of gods, these deliverers of all that is good. I first mentioned this phenomenon on my radio show a few months ago. Not only was I deluged with callers co-signing my experience, but for weeks afterward I received tons of e-mails from other Roker Effect veterans and even a few rookies. That's right, some people actually tested my hypothesis themselves and were shocked to find out that it's true.

Do it yourself. Go on. Put this down and go to the TV. Scan the channels, find a fat, black weatherman, and relax. In seconds you'll transcend to a lofty dimension that before seemed only the purview of maharishis.

Seriously, go ahead, I'll wait.

Take your time.

Go.

You're back. What'd you think? Fucking awesome, wasn't it? I told you. What's amazing is that it pretty much works for everybody. Some have dismissed this as just the effect of the personality of the particular meteorologist. Others have suggested a cultural sociological component at work. Let's take a look at both.

I agree that fat, black weathermen have great personalities and that some are actually quite witty and downright funny. But this explains only why they can make me laugh, not why they make me feel happy.

For instance, many times Al Roker conducts interviews on the *Today* show. This is usually after the nine o'clock hour when the format of the show loosens up a bit. Mr. Roker is always very charming in his interviews. He normally appears well informed. He's almost always passionate about even the dullest subject. He even manages to squeeze laughs out of situations where there shouldn't be any.

Meh. Who cares? I'm smiling but I'm not happy. I'm filled with bemusement but not with joy. He did a lot to inform me but nothing to transform me. However I felt before he started his little interview is exactly how I feel now. So it's not personality.

What about the cultural component? Let's take a look.

I had a college professor e-mail me with a theory about sociological guilt playing a part. He opined that because our culture is so used to blacks being treated poorly, it makes us feel good when they are doing well. Well, then why aren't we happy when they deliver the news? Because, he explains, if he has too much authority we feel a bit threatened. Conversely, if he's doing sports, we feel patronized. Weather is a good neutral area that makes everybody feel good without triggering any incendiary racial history.

Bullshit.

First of all, this explains only the alleviation of guilt. It does not explain why his weather report makes my body produce serotonin. Plus, this examines the phenomenon only from a white viewer's point of view. I'm black and he makes me feel happy every time! And don't forget, I peed pants of joy for Big Johnny Page when I was just a toddler! Explain that, sociology man!

No, the real reason black weathermen make me feel happy, especially the fat ones, can be summed up in one word: "magic."

It's magic when they stand in front of that map of the

United States with all those squiggly lines, pictures of suns and clouds, and numbers that are never right.

It's magic when they explain highs and lows, fronts and swells, desert Santa Anas, and coastal eddies.

It's magic when they warn of coming tornadoes, impending hurricanes, and gale force winds.

It's magic when they chuckle about extreme wind chills and Indian summers.

It's magic when they "throw" it to my part of town, or my neighborhood, or my neck of the woods.

It's magic when they laugh at their own jokes, put the anchors in their places, and are first to eat the guest chef's barbecue.

It's magic when they hold that little clicker and change their background to match what they're saying.

It's magic when, at the conclusion of their segment, I start applauding. Not because they're good. Not because they're entertaining. Not because I'm proud and not because I feel sorry for them. I applaud because they made me feel happy. And they do it every time.

Especially the fat ones.

Black Weathermen Make Me Feel Sad

After writing how black weathermen made him feel happy, it appears Wilmore had a change of heart.

I turn on the news, the lead story is always something tragic. Someone was raped, killed, or both. Something or someone blew up in the Middle East. People are starving somewhere far and near. Families are losing homes and homes are losing families. Stock prices go down as oil prices go up. There are pesticides in our foods, suicides in our schools, and genocides in Darfurs. The bad guys in the world have found another way to win and my home team has found another way to lose. It's not even fifteen past the hour and I feel so down that a double

Prozac with a selective serotonin reuptake inhibitor chaser couldn't rescue me from an imploding sense of ennui. Enter the black weatherman. Why Lord?

Black weathermen make me feel sad. I don't care how bad the story is before it gets "thrown" to them. They make me even more depressed. I don't know if they're doing it on purpose, if they're aware of it, or if it's just some perverse gift they all share. All I know is, I can't stand them. And the fat ones make me feel worse than the skinny ones.

I'm not saying I frown at their stupid jokes or find their overdependence on puns to be brain numbing. I'm saying they make me feel sad. Like I said, especially the fat ones.

Do weathermen make me feel sad? Not necessarily. Do black newsmen make me feel sad? I don't think so. Do fat black people in general on TV make me feel sad? Not in any way I can measure. It's the debilitating combination of black, weather, and fat that kills the endorphins locked in my brain. I like to call it the Reverse Roker Effect.

Al Roker has a gift. He was the first fat black weatherman—that I can recall—to lift my spirits. Though my mother recounts an incident that occurred during my toddler years when I always seemed to wet my diaper whenever they had the news on. It seems I was so happy, I peed my pants. Mom attributed the phenomenon to my love of television or even news. I felt it went deeper and after a little research was proven correct.

Apparently, back in the mid-sixties, our local TV station was one of the first to feature a fat black weatherman. His name was Big Johnny Page and he did the weather for the six o'clock news. I looked him up online and upon seeing his picture, immediately wet my pants.

Think about it. Even after over forty years, the mere sight of this zoftig atmosphere prognosticator filled me with so much joy, my bladder had to empty to make room.

Anyway, this is commonly known as the Roker Effect. Unfortunately, the effect doesn't last long and the temporary happiness I feel is replaced by a tidal wave of unbearable sadness. This is the Reverse Roker. I also realize that wetting myself was not an expression of uncontainable joy but of overflowing emotional distress.

I'm not alone, by the way. Many have reported this same depression when in the electronic presence of one of these evil humans, these sons of satan, these deliverers of all that is bad.

I first mentioned this phenomenon on my radio show a few months ago. Not only was I deluged with callers co-signing my experience, but for weeks afterward I received tons of e-mails from other Reverse Roker Effect veterans and even a few rookies. That's right, some people actually tested my hypothesis themselves and were shocked to find out that it's true.

Do it yourself. Go on. Put this down and go to the TV. Scan the channels, find a fat, black weatherman, and relax. In seconds you'll transcend to a depth of sorrow that before seemed only the purview of beotches.

Seriously, go ahead, I'll wait.

Take your time.

Go.

You're back. What'd you think? Fucking pathetic, wasn't it? I told you. What's amazing is that it pretty much works for everybody. Some have dismissed this as just the effect of the personality of the particular meteorologist. Others have suggested a cultural sociological component at work. Let's take a look at both.

I agree that fat, black weathermen have great personalities and that some are actually quite witty and downright funny. As if they're overcompensating for their shame of being a weatherman by telling jokes. Well, this explains only why I feel sorry for them not why they make me sad.

For instance, many times Al Roker conducts interviews on the *Today* show. This is usually after the nine o'clock hour, when the format of the show loosens up a bit. Mr. Roker is always very charming in his interviews. He normally appears well informed. He's almost always passionate about even the dullest subject. He even manages to squeeze laughs out of situations where there shouldn't be any.

Meh. Who cares? I'm bored but I'm not sad. If anything I'm angry. If he's so entertaining now, why isn't he good enough to be doing interviews before nine o'clock? Between seven and nine a.m., we want the brother telling us only if it's hot or cold and making us laugh. Like I said, angry but not sad. So, it's not personality.

What about the cultural component? Let's take a look.

I had a college professor e-mail me with a theory about sociological guilt playing a part. He opined that because our culture is so used to blacks being treated poorly, it makes us feel sad when they are finally doing well. Well, then why aren't we sad when they deliver the news? Because, he explains, if he's in a position of power, we feel proud. Conversely, if he's doing sports, he's probably an ex-athlete and we already like him. Weather is an unfortunate middle ground that makes everybody feel sad without triggering any incendiary racial history.

Bullshit.

First of all, this explains only why I pity him. It does not explain why his weather report makes my body incapable of producing serotonin. Plus, this examines the phenomenon from only a white viewer's point of view. I'm black and he makes me feel sad every time! And don't forget, I peed pants of pain for Big Johnny

Page when I was just a toddler! Explain that, sociology man!

No, the real reason black weathermen make me feel sad, especially the fat ones, can be summed up in one word: "tragic."

It's tragic when they stand in front of that map of the United States with all those squiggly lines, pictures of suns and clouds, and numbers that are never right.

It's tragic when they explain highs and lows, fronts and swells, desert Santa Anas, and coastal eddies.

It's tragic when they warn of coming tornadoes, impending hurricanes, and gale force winds.

It's tragic when they chuckle about extreme wind chills and Indian summers.

It's tragic when they "throw" it to my part of town, or my neighborhood, or my neck of the woods.

It's tragic when they laugh at their own jokes, put the anchors in their places, and are the first to eat the guest chef's barbecue.

It's tragic when they hold that little clicker that changes their background to match what they're saying.

It's tragic when, at the conclusion of their segments, I start tearing up. Not because they're bad. Not because they're pathetic. Not because I'm proud and not because I feel sorry for them. I tear up because they make me feel sad. And they do it every time.

Especially the fat ones.

Random Black
Thought #1

Changing of the Guard

Queen Latifah has officially become Pearl Bailey.

How Come Brothas Don't See UFOs? PART I

*W*ilmore was fascinated with the possibility of extraterrestrials and life on other planets. He said he had planned to do a television special on the topic but never got around to it. You can really see his passion come through in the following op-ed.

On April 16, 1987, in a small rural town on the outskirts of Mariposa County, California, a small band of UFOs was seen by 99.9 percent of the residents in the balmy night sky. They were able to faithfully recall the shape and movements of the mysterious crafts with incredible uniformity. "A cluster of small silent black triangles flying in formation" was the way most of them put it. The local news reported the event, the townspeople discussed it daily for nearly a year, and even a few major newspapers covered the story. Most were impressed by the clarity of the recollections. Some were blown away by the grainy amateur video. A few were taken by the astounding 99.9 percent close encounter rate. I was more interested in the .1 percent that didn't see the UFO. That .1 percent was named Clerow Mims: the only black resident of the city.

How come brothas don't see UFOs? I have asked this question for the last thirty years and have yet to stumble upon any satisfactory answer. UFOs have been sighted almost everywhere on earth for the last sixty years and I can't recall even one sighting by a brotha. How is this possible? Is it a conspiracy on the part of the UFOs? Are aliens racist? Or is it something about brothas themselves that don't allow them to have this experience? After numerous interviews with experts and exhaustive research, I've arrived at a few possible theories.

HISTORY

Brothas automatically block out anything or anybody that might want to take them for a ride on a ship for an indeterminate amount of time.

MELANIN

Many ufologists have theorized that we are able to see aliens because of a light signal that is emitted from the ship and is reflected off our skin. This makes them visible to the human eye. Unfortunately, blacks have an abundance of melanin in their skin, which acts like stealth technology and absorbs the signal, rendering UFOs invisible.

The upside of this phenomenom is that light-skinned brothas might have a better chance of seeing aliens than dark-skinned.

STREET CRED

Brothas could be afraid to report UFO sightings for fear of losing street cred. Street cred is hard to come by. Many times you have to get shot to obtain a decent amount of street cred. Would you really want all of that erased just because you saw something that you can't explain flying in the sky? I don't think so.

REDUNDANCY

Most people think if aliens arrived on earth, they would take over and rule us all. In other words, they would become the Man. That's all brothas need, so what's the point? They may as well have spotted a cop.

IT'S NOT A BIG ENOUGH CONSPIRACY

Alien life, as a conspiracy theory, is nothing compared to some of the shit brothas come up with. In fact, some black liberationist religions teach that white people are aliens who inhabited the earth thousands of years ago (I'm not making this up).

BROTHAS ARE JUST THAT UNLUCKY

Most brothas accept this theory and chalk it up to the same odds they have of winning the lottery: slim to none.

BROTHAS MIGHT ACTUALLY BE ALIENS

Not a bad theory. It would explain a lot.

BROTHAS ARE AFRAID OF ALIENS

Some aliens have been called snake people for their reptilian-like features. Everybody knows brothas are afraid of snakes, so this theory carries a high degree of probablility.

BROTHAS DON'T LIKE HOSPITALS

What does this have to do with aliens? Simple. Almost all alien abduction stories include lying on an operating table and being cut open. Brothas won't even go to a hospital to pick up a paycheck, let alone for surgery. And when you include the fact that these alien operations seem to always end with an unpleasant anal probe, you can count brothas out.

IT'S A GOVERNMENT CONSPIRACY

It's possible that brothas have seen UFOs and have reported them but the government, for whatever reason, has covered it up. It's not too far fetched. The government is already covering up the existence of aliens, why wouldn't they cover up the record of brothas reporting their existence?

Though all of these theories are legitimate, it's the last one that intrigues me the most. What if there is a governmental cover-up at work? What if there are fantastic stories of brothas and UFOs that the government just didn't want us to know about? I don't know if these questions can ever be answered satisfactorily. But one thing is for sure, if brothas have seen strange lights in the sky that were not police helicopters, I'm going to make sure the world knows.

Talk-Back Trauma

*E*verybody knows black people talk back to the movies. What people don't know is that this incessant peanut gallery chatter can sometimes have an adverse effect on the characters on-screen. One of the most unusual interviews from Wilmore's radio show was the time he spoke to several of these characters. Their stories were moving and Wilmore was clearly touched by their visit.

WILMORE: That's where I bought my Lexus and you can too. Just ask for the friendly people at Circle Lexus. Tell them you heard this ad on *The Larry Wilmore Show*. (Show music.) Welcome back to *The Larry Wilmore Show*, I'm Larry Wilmore

and today we have an unusual lineup of guests in
our studio. They are all characters from movies
who all share a common . . . affliction, I guess you
could say. Anyway, I'll let them tell you all about
it. Please welcome Girl #1 from the horror movie
Screwdriver 3, Janitor from the sci-fi thriller *Vaccident,* and Man in Crosswalk from the action
film *Carpool of Blood.* Thank you all for being on
the show. Girl #1, tell us why you're here and
what kind of ties you all together.

GIRL #1: Sure. As Larry said, I'm Girl #1 from *Screwdriver 3—*

WILMORE: You're the actor who played Girl #1?

GIRL #1: No, I'm the actual character Girl #1. We're
all the characters from our films, not the actors
who played us.

WILMORE: Oh, okay. That's unusual. Go ahead.

GIRL #1: Well, we are all suffering from talk-back
trauma.

WILMORE: Talk-back trauma, is that a scientific term?

GIRL #1: No, it's a colloquial term that we use to describe the condition of not being able to perform in certain theaters.

WILMORE: Meaning you're not able to appear in movies you're supposed to be in because of this condition?

GIRL #1: Exactly.

WILMORE: And what causes this trauma?

GIRL #1: It's caused by people yelling at us from the audience.

WILMORE: You mean like "Don't go in there" or—

All three guests react in unison.

ALL: Hey, don't say that. Ow.

WILMORE: Sorry. I guess you're pretty sensitive about that.

JANITOR: Yes, we are, Larry.

WILMORE: Could you introduce yourself?

JANITOR: Yes, I'm Janitor from the movie *Vaccident*. Larry, I get killed off three minutes after the credits and all I hear is "Don't go in there, don't go in there!" Well, you know what, they got their fucking wish, I'm not going in there ever again. Sorry about that.

WILMORE: That's okay, we're on delay. I can see you have a lot of passion about this.

JANITOR: Absolutely.

WILMORE: Is it the same for you, Man in Crosswalk?

MAN IN CROSSWALK: Almost. Since I get hit by a car, it's always "Watch out, watch out." And then after I'm killed, it's always "Stupid m-f," or something like that.

WILMORE: Really?

MAN IN CROSSWALK: Oh, yeah. And that's just the nice stuff.

GIRL #1: At least they warn you. As the screwdriver is being bored through my skull, all I hear is "Look at that stupid bitch" or "Get that bitch."

WILMORE: Wow. That is shocking. And this happens whenever your movie is shown?

GIRL #1: Oh no. Only in front of black audiences.

WILMORE: You're kidding. Janitor?

JANITOR: Black audiences.

WILMORE: Man in Crosswalk?

MAN IN CROSSWALK: Yep, black audiences. Sometimes I hear it from senior citizens but I get the sense that they're just trying to be helpful.

WILMORE: I see. So, none of you will show up in your films anymore?

ALL: No.

JANITOR: I don't even want to be downloaded to a black household. If you think they talk a lot in the theater, they just won't shut up at home.

WILMORE: Let me see if I understand this correctly. You're in a film that's already been shot. How can you suddenly not appear in a scene, how is that possible?

GIRL #1: I don't understand the technological stuff, I can only speak about the emotional. And frankly, I'm a mess.

MAN IN CROSSWALK: Amen.

JANITOR: I don't even like showing up for the credits.

WILMORE: Okay, well, this sounds pretty serious and I'm sure my audience would like to hear more but we're going to take a little break and when we come back we'll explore some of the cultural aspects of this phenomenon and we'll take some of your calls. You're listening to *The Larry Wilmore Show*. (Show music.)

WILMORE: (Show music.) And we're back. This is Larry Wilmore and I'm speaking today to a few characters from some popular films who have experienced talk-back trauma. That is a condition that comes from being continually berated by audiences.

JANITOR: Black audiences, Larry.

WILMORE: Okay, now, you bring up an interesting point. Is there a racial component here? I mean, why do you think black people like to talk back to the screen?

GIRL #1: The long answer is there could be a sense of community in the movie theater felt by blacks that other groups don't share. Or maybe they're afraid of the dark and this is their way of coping. The short answer is, I don't care. Stop it.

WILMORE: Interesting. Have any of you ever experienced this before? In other movies.

MAN IN CROSSWALK: My cousin was the brother who was killed thirty seconds into *Jurassic Park*. They were still yelling at him halfway through the movie.

JANITOR: Your cousin was Worker #1?

MAN IN CROSSWALK: Mm-hmm.

JANITOR: He was good.

MAN IN CROSSWALK: Thank you.

WILMORE: So, they told him not to go in there?

MAN IN CROSSWALK: Right. And, granted, he should not have taken his black ass in there. Number one, it was a velociraptor for chrissakes and number two, everybody knows the brotha gets killed in the beginning of all those movies.

GIRL #1: See, Larry, that's the thing, he knew he was going to be killed. He didn't need all those black people making him feel stupid about it.

WILMORE: Right, right, they're just killing a dead horse.

MAN IN CROSSWALK: Exactly.

WILMORE: Okay, well let's take some calls and see what the audience is thinking. Judy, you're on *The Larry Wilmore Show*.

JUDY: Hi, Larry, I love your show.

WILMORE: Thank you.

JUDY: My question is for Janitor. I saw *Vaccident* and I have to admit when I saw you opening the door to the lab, I knew you were going to get stabbed with that hypodermic needle and I wanted to tell you not to go in there but I didn't say anything.

JANITOR: Appreciate it.

JUDY: I want to know, why did you go in there? I mean, weren't you suspicious at all, especially after the assistant was killed in the scene before?

JANITOR: Well, it doesn't really matter because I have to do what the script says. I'm a character in the film and I'm supposed to get killed in that scene or else the story doesn't move forward.

JUDY: I know, but I felt kind of guilty. Like maybe if I had said something you might not have gone in there and you wouldn't have been vaccinated.

JANITOR: I don't think you understand, I have to go in there. It's in the script, it's been shot, it has to happen that way.

JUDY: I know, I know, I completely understand. It's just that, maybe, if you had some kind of warning he was there, I'm just saying—

WILMORE: It sounds like she feels pretty bad about not being able to help you. Do you find people yell at the screen because they honestly want to be of assistance?

JANITOR: It's possible, but it really doesn't matter. There're so many people yelling at you, all you can do is try to shut it out and do the scene.

WILMORE: All right, Manny, you're on *The Larry Wilmore Show*.

MANNY: Hey Larry, long-time listener, first-time caller.

WILMORE: Thank you. Do you have a question for our guests?

MANNY: Yes, I do. As a Latino, I would like to know, how do you handle it when people shout in different languages? Because in the movie theaters I go to, everybody's yelling in Spanish.

WILMORE: Great question, Manny. Does yelling at the screen in a different language affect you the same?

MAN IN CROSSWALK: Not really. It's been mostly black people who speak English with me. I'm not dubbed in any other language, so if someone has yelled in Spanish, I didn't understand it.

GIRL #1: I'm dubbed in three languages but other than English, I've only experienced black people yelling at me in French.

WILMORE: Black people in France yell at the movie screen?

JANITOR: Black people everywhere yell at the movie screen.

WILMORE: Have any of you ever taken their advice and not gone in there?

GIRL #1: No, but once somebody told me to talk louder and I said my lines softer instead.

WILMORE: Really? What happened?

GIRL #1: He said, "I still can't hear you" and then someone else from the audience told him that if he shut up then all of them could hear me. Everybody cheered and he shut up.

WILMORE: That's cool. You won them over to your side.

GIRL #1: Not for long. By the next scene, even the person who came to my defense was calling me a dumb beotch.

WILMORE: Such a cruel thing to say.

GIRL #1: Actually, my character is a dumb beotch. I just don't want two hundred black people screaming it at me all the time.

MAN IN CROSSWALK: I flipped somebody off once.

WILMORE: You're kidding. I want to hear about that and more of your calls when we return. You're listening to *The Larry Wilmore Show*. (Show music.)

WILMORE: (Show music.) And welcome back to *The Larry Wilmore Show*. Today we are talking to a group of characters from films who've been traumatized by being yelled at by black audiences. Man in Crosswalk, you were about to share a story before the break?

MAN IN CROSSWALK: Yes, it was an afternoon showing in Pasadena, California, and there was only one black guy in the audience and sure enough, he wouldn't stop talking back to the screen. My scene was coming up and I'm thinking I gotta do something this time. I'm not just going to play the scene and pretend like I don't hear him. So after he called me stupid for the fourth time, I flipped him the bird. I looked right at him too. A couple of people got it and started laughing, but he looked a little shaken. He came back a few days later with some friends and you should've seen his face when I didn't flip him off. I think he suspected what had happened and was coming back to prove it to himself.

WILMORE: What a great story. Let's go to Derek; you're on *The Larry Wilmore Show*.

DEREK: Hey Larry, good job as always.

WILMORE: Thank you.

DEREK: Um, I believe what your guests are saying and I accept that they might be a little emotionally damaged, but this all sounds a little racist to me.

WILMORE: Derek, are you African-American?

DEREK: Yes, I am, Larry, and I've never yelled or talked back to a movie screen in my life.

Wilmore: Is there any racism involved here?

Janitor: I don't think so, Larry. First of all, I'm black. Second, you could ask any killed-off tertiary character from almost any slasher flick and they will tell you it's the black audiences that give them the hardest time. I'm not saying other people don't do it a little, I'm saying black people do it in spades. No pun intended.

Wilmore: I see your point. I guess we have to take your word on that.

Derek: Take his word? How're you going to take his word? He was too stupid to not listen to us when we told him not to go in there and get his black ass vaccinated to turn him into a zombie! How is he smart enough now to tell me these statements aren't racist?

Janitor: "When we told him"? I thought you said you never talked back at a movie?

Derek: I was using the colloquial "we." Don't try to trip me up. You know your stupid ass never should've gone in there and all of y'all are trying to pass the buck to us because you were too dumb to listen.

JANITOR: It's not real! It's a movie! If I don't "go in there," there won't be a freaking film! Can't you people get that through your heads? Stop telling us what to do!

There's a short silence.

DEREK: Larry, you need to check your boy. (Abrupt dial tone.)

WILMORE: Well, that certainly got a little heated. We're almost out of time but before I let my guests go I have to ask, what's next? Girl #1?

GIRL #1: I feel all I can do at this time is to keep speaking out to let people know. I appreciate you having us on your show, Larry, so our message can get out.

WILMORE: And that message is?

GIRL #1: Black people, when you're watching a film, watch it. That's all you should be doing. Leave the commentary to the critics.

WILMORE: Well said. Janitor?

JANITOR: Personally, I refuse to appear in black theaters until something changes.

WILMORE: You won't appear at all?

JANITOR: Nope. They're just going to have to cut around me.

WILMORE: Wow. Man in Crosswalk, what about you?

MAN IN CROSSWALK: I've decided I'm going to start listening.

WILMORE: Listening? Really?

MAN IN CROSSWALK: Oh yeah. If black people don't want me to cross the street, I'm not going to cross the street.

WILMORE: But couldn't that change the whole outcome of the movie?

MAN IN CROSSWALK: Larry, I don't care. Maybe if I listen to them, they'll say some nice things about me.

JANITOR: Good luck.

WILMORE: Yes, good luck to all of you. I'd like to thank all of my guests today. Girl #1 from the movie *Screwdriver 3*, Janitor from *Vaccident*, and Man in Crosswalk from *Carpool of Blood*. In full disclosure, I should admit that I saw the movie *Vaccident* and I'm sorry, but I told you not to go in there too.

JANITOR: Motherfu—

End of show.

A Second Letter
to the NAACP

This is Wilmore's second attempt trying to convince the NAACP to adopt "chocolate" as the new designation for African-Americans.

Dear Sir,

I'm following up on an e-mail I sent you last month about changing our name to chocolate. I haven't heard back from you and I wanted to make sure you got it. I attached it onto the end of this note along with my original essay.

Since that time, I've really been giving "chocolate" a test run. I use it in almost every conversation I have. No matter what the topic,

I twist it around to the subject of race. As soon as someone says something like, "I think it's great when African-Americans blah, blah, blah," I'll answer with something like, "All of the chocolate people I know would never blah, blah, blah . . ." Then they say, "Chocolate?" And I say, "Yeah, chocolate, come on." I make them feel like "how dare they don't know we have a new name" and it's done. Next thing you know, they're using it. It's fucking awesome! (Excuse my French.)

I really think you should give it a try. Even if you're not ready for casual conversation, there are a lot of other opportunities to get the point across. Here are just a few I've tried:

PUT IT ON YOUR TAX FORM

I did this on my last return and no one blinked an eye. In the space where it says "other," put "chocolate." Or, better yet, do what I did and cross out "African-American" and replace it with "chocolate." This is a nice statement that goes directly to the government. And government employees are way too touchy-feely and oversensitive to do anything about it.

CHANGE YOUR BIRTH CERTIFICATE

This is great because many birth certificates have a line for "ancestry" instead of "race." Come on now, how cool is it to be from "chocolate" ancestry?

USE IT ON YOUR ONLINE PROFILE

This is a great way to get the fire started. So far, I've changed my racial profile to "chocolate" on Facebook, MySpace, hi5, LinkedIn, Match.com, and Divorcedmiddleagedsingleswithkids whoarentbitter.com. Now all of my "friends" on Facebook are "chocolate" lovers and I've gotten twice as many bites on Divorcedmiddleaged singleswithkidswhoarentbitter.com since the change. (No dates though ☹.)

CHANGE YOUR DRIVER'S LICENSE

This is good because not only does it serve as a "proving" tool for people who don't believe you're chocolate, it also forces cops who pull you over for a DWB to describe you that way. For example, when you get pulled over in Beverly Hills and they pull your license they have to say, "I've got a chocolate male, six foot two, approximately 220 pounds, blah, blah, blah . . ." Tell me that's not a bonus.

GET MAD IF PEOPLE DON'T CALL YOU CHOCOLATE

This is one of the most effective ways to change the mind-set. White people are always uncomfortable around angry brothas. When they see your anger subside by their use of "chocolate," that's a win-win all the way around. This works on brothas too.

CALL WHITE PEOPLE VANILLA

This is not as risky as it sounds. White people are very cool when black people give them pet names and vanilla is already one of their favorites. Heck, one of the most famous white rappers was Vanilla Ice, so you know they already like it. Plus, it lowers their level of tension when they call you chocolate, in case they had some reservations. Try it.

Anyhow, these are just some of my methods. I'm sure you've probably already thought of some.

I can't stress enough how important it is for us to get your imprimatur on this cause. Your support means a lot. Please let me know what you think. Once again, you can reach me on my cell. (I have a new number so don't call the old one.)

Take care, and I look forward to hearing from you.

Your "Milk Chocolate" Brotha,
Larry Wilmore
(new cell: 818-555-5393)
(chocolate5800612.pdf 135kb)
(letter8790011.pdf 28kb) attached

Eulogy for the "N" Word

O   *ne of Wilmore's more infamous public appear-*
ances was at the symbolic funeral for the "n" word.
This was an event staged by several civil rights groups
about a year ago. Many felt the word was too caustic to be
used anymore. There was so much hurt and bad history
surrounding it that the only proper thing was to kill it
from use and then bury it publicly so people would know
that it really was dead. Apparently Wilmore delivered the
eulogy for the "n" word. Though there is no written
record of it, luckily someone present recorded it and gave
me the transcripts.

(The descriptions and observations in the paragraphs
were made by me from what I could ascertain from the
recording.)

The crowd has just finished singing "We Shall Over-come" while holding hands. Before that, there were brief words from someone who sounded like the Rev. Jesse Jackson. I didn't hear any rhyming so I can't be a hundred percent certain. We can hear Wilmore take the loudspeaker (I think it was a bullhorn) and start the "sermon."

WILMORE: Brothers and sisters. We are gathered here today to say good-bye.

CROWD: That's right.

WILMORE: To say good-bye to someone whose time has come.

CROWD: Time has come.

WILMORE: To say good-bye to someone with a complicated past.

CROWD: Complicated.

WILMORE: Checkered, some might say. Controversial, I've heard from others. Hurtful, I've heard from most.

CROWD: Hurtful. Very hurtful.

WILMORE: We may not agree about its past but we are certain of its future. Ashes to ashes, dust to dust. Can I get a response?

CROWD: Amen.

WILMORE: He's off to meet his maker. And by maker, I'm referring to the dead slave owner who's shaking hands with Satan by the gates of hell— somebody interrupt me with a hallelujah!

CROWD: Hallelujah!

The crowd cheers. Wilmore seems pretty good at this and starts to find his stride. Although I get the impression most people were unsure why he was continuing.

WILMORE: Now, before we lay him down for his eternal rest, I've got a confession to make.

The crowd murmurs.

WILMORE: I say I've got a confession to make. Something heavy is lying on my heart.

CROWD: Get it off! Confess!

WILMORE: I shall, brothers and sisters, I shall.

You can now sense the crowd is getting a little uncomfortable during Wilmore's pregnant pause.

WILMORE: I sense this vile word, a word so vile, in fact, we have to call it by its acronym—the "n" word—is not quite dead.

The crowd reacts confused.

WILMORE: In fact, I might go so far as to say I can feel it trembling on the edge of my own lips.

CROWD: No, no.

WILMORE: Yes. This satanic word that is the root of much suffering for our people, I fear is about to come out of my mouth right now. Ni—

CROWD: No, no, don't do it.

Wilmore is now working himself up like a revivalist preacher. The crowd has caught on and gets into the spirit with a call and response reaction.

Wilmore: I can't help it, I'm too weak. I thought this word was dead. I thought we killed it. I thought it was on its way to a fiery grave, but I must be mistaken because while the spirit of the Lord is trying to keep my mouth closed, the designs of the devil are trying to break me down!

Crowd: Be strong.

Wilmore: Lord help me, I'm gonna say it.

Crowd: No.

Wilmore: I'm gonna say it.

Crowd: No!

Wilmore: I gotta say it!

Crowd: No, you don't!

Wilmore: Yes, I do. If I don't say it now, if I don't kill it for good, it's going to find a way back. Did you hear me, I said it's going to find a way back!

Crowd: No.

WILMORE: Yes. I gotta kill it so it doesn't come back. I gotta kill it, so it doesn't haunt our people anymore. I gotta kill it so not even Jesus could resurrect it! Tell me what I gotta do!

CROWD: You gotta kill it!

WILMORE: I don't want this word in my conversations anymore! Tell me what I gotta do!

CROWD: You gotta kill it!

WILMORE: I don't want this word in my music anymore! Tell me what I gotta do!

CROWD: You gotta kill it!

WILMORE: I don't want this word in my off-color jokes anymore! Tell me what I gotta do!

CROWD: You gotta kill it!

WILMORE: I don't want this word in the rosy rearview mirror of my memories anymore! Tell me what I gotta do!

CROWD: You gotta kill it!

WILMORE: Not in the classroom.

CROWD: Kill it!

WILMORE: Not in the car.

CROWD: Kill it!

WILMORE: Not in the shower.

CROWD: Kill it!

WILMORE: Not when I stub my toe.

CROWD: Kill it!

WILMORE: Not in the barber shop.

CROWD: Kill it!

WILMORE: Not with Sam I Am.

CROWD: Kill it!

WILMORE: Not even in the recesses of my mind!
　　Lord tell me what I gotta do!

CROWD: You gotta kill it!

WILMORE: I gotta kill it.

Wilmore seems out of breath. Everyone is on pins and needles.

WILMORE: I think it's passed. Wait. Yes, I think it's passed. I don't feel it anymore. I think we killed it.

CROWD: Praise God!

WILMORE: Yes. It really is dead now.

The crowd cheers.

You can feel the emotions of the crowd from the recording. Wilmore really took a staid symbolic march and turned it into something special. He made the people feel like they had actually killed the "n" word, like a Catholic priest exorcising a demon. It would've been a perfect ceremony, but after the burial someone handed a spent Wilmore a bottle of water. After taking a sip he poured a bit onto the "n" word grave. The crowd seemed confused and asked him what he was doing.

WILMORE: Oh. That's for the niggas that aren't here.

• • •

This is where the recording stops. You could hear what sounded like a man screaming before it cut off. It sounded a bit like Wilmore but I could be mistaken. All in all, a fascinating account that in many ways mirrors Wilmore's career. Just when he seemed to have everyone's ear, he says the wrong thing and disappears as if he were never there.

Random Black Thought #2

Tan Lines

Yes, brothas do get tan lines.

In Search of Black Jesus

*W*ilmore explores the clues in the Bible that may prove the existence of a black Jesus.

For many blacks, the question of whether or not Jesus was black is not a provocative issue. They cite the passage in the Bible that refers to Christ's olive skin and wool-like hair as evidence. Though this is enough to satiate the most ardent of conspiracy theorists, I find it lacking. At the most, it describes only the features of a man that were probably very common in that region. It does little to answer the vital question of true and authentic blackness. After all, the issue is not whether Jesus was dark but whether he was black.

I've taken it upon myself to look at other clues in the

Scripture. Clues that may give us a sense of not just his true hue but his homey heritage. I think you'll find I've made my case.

CLUE #1: *From the moment of the immaculate conception, the question of "who the baby daddy" was already an issue.*

I'm not saying this makes Jesus black, but without DNA testing in his time and no existence of a Maury Povich show, this open question *brothafies* him in my book.

CLUE #2: *He was born in a manger because his parents weren't allowed to stay in any inn.*

Weren't allowed because they were . . . you can finish it.

CLUE #3: *His cousin had the first hip-hop name: John the Baptist.*

This is a good two thousand years before Cedric the Entertainer.

CLUE #4: *He walked on water.*

There's only one reason he would choose to walk on water. Brothas can't swim.

CLUE #5: *He spoke in pre-Ebonics.*

Blessed *be* the poor, blessed *be* the meek, etc., etc.

These were even called the *be*atitudes. That's a double bonus. It takes the black familiar use of "be" and couples it with "attitude." And this doesn't even take into account all the *be*gats.

CLUE #6: *He had a large posse.*

Even by today's standards a twelve-man posse is pretty big. In fact, some suggest the word "posse" is derived from "apostle."

CLUE #7: *He turned water into wine.*

On the surface, this may not seem black but the original texts suggest he actually turned water into wine *cooler.* Obviously a brotha move. To further prove the point, "Blessed is he who wants to get this party started" was deleted from the Gospel of John at the Second Council of Constantinople in 553 A.D.

CLUE #8: *He fed five thousand with two loaves and five fish.*

There is only one way to do this: make gumbo. I've seen brothas who started with less feed more than five thousand.

CLUE #9: *He cured a man of leprosy.*

Wait a minute, Larry, how does this make him black? It's simple: the Hebrew for leprosy allows for many skin conditions. It's more likely the person had ashy elbows or razor bumps. Only a black Jesus would've noticed such a thing. There's evidence he gave him an early form of cocoa butter.

CLUE #10: *He drank out of a chalice.*

Once again, he did this a good two thousand years before Snoop Dogg made it cool.

CLUE #11: *He didn't have a job.*

We all know Jesus was a carpenter but there's no historical evidence to suggest that he ever had a job. Keep in mind, this was back in the day when everything was either wood or stone. It would seem to me that if you were a carpenter, you'd be turning down work pretty much your whole life. The fact that there's no evidence Jesus ever had a job in thirty-three years can be attributed only to racism. No one wanted to hire a brotha carpenter.

CLUE #12: *He may have been involved with a white girl.*

There's a very large following of believers who insist Jesus and Mary Magdalene may have been married and at the least might've had an affair. Here's my take. You're the son of God, the prince of peace, the most important person to ever walk the earth **and** you're black. Of course, you're going to have a white girl.

CLUE #13: *He had street cred.*

Yeah, he was born poor. Yeah, he didn't have a job. Yeah, he had a white girlfriend. But Jesus never really took off till one of his posse betrayed him and had him killed. Instant street cred.

CLUE #14: *Like Tupac, he became more famous after he died.*

And also like Tupac, years after his death, fresh material is still being unearthed.

CLUE #15: *He didn't get a fair trial.*

Nuff said.

CLUE #16: *The Romans cast lots to see who would get his garments.*

Lots were an early form of the game craps. Why would they do this in front of Jesus and no one else?

CLUE #17: *He rose from the dead in three days.*

Why not two, or one, or instantly? Obviously, he was on cp time.

CLUE #18: *People wear bling around their necks in honor of him.*

Even people you would not qualify as being particularly brotha-friendly honor a black Jesus in this way.

CLUE #19: *No one knows where he is.*

He said he'd be back but no one's seen him for two thousand years. If this isn't like a brother, then I don't know what.

These clues are just the beginning. There's a lot more evidence to prove the existence of a black Jesus but I will leave it up to you to find it. In your quest, I will only remind you to keep an open mind and to keep it real.

Give Us the Superdome

*W*ilmore makes a case for reparations in this post-Katrina op-ed.

Much has been said about reparations for blacks in this country and much has been left unsaid. Is it fair to give people money for something that happened almost 150 years ago? And if you could make a case for it, how do you determine how much and to whom? There are many blacks whose ancestors aren't necessarily linked to American slavery. Is it fair that they get a piece? And who pays for this? Is it right to ask today's taxpayers to make good on a bill they had nothing to do with? And won't we be building up new resentments? There are groups who immigrated to this country after slavery and are really caught in the middle. Why should they pick up the tab?

The answer to all of these questions is, you're right. It's too late. Forty acres and a mule were supposed to be the reparations. When the government failed to deliver on that promise, we should've been given our proper due. Unfortunately, racism reared its ugly head and buried the promissory notes. After 150 years, we can't expect reparations to have a longer statute of limitations than murder. So, the answer to reparations is to link it to a more recent indiscretion. Enter Hurricane Katrina.

This one storm did more damage to governmental race relations than to the levees it breached. Blacks felt abandoned, forgotten, marginalized, abused, and discarded like trash. They begged for food and water on cable TV as *Air Force One* flew by overhead with a galley full of Fiji and Funyuns.

No one could argue that the government shouldn't give blacks some sort of recompense, or reparations if you will, for this unspeakable treatment. Should it be cash? No, it's too hard to agree on a figure that would please everyone. My solution is very simple: give us the Superdome.

But Larry, isn't the Superdome privately owned? I don't care. Claim eminent domain and give it to us. It's the least you can do. Now you could assert that why should all blacks get the Superdome when it affected only those in New Orleans? Fine. All the black people in New Orleans affected by Hurricane Katrina get the Superdome. I got no problem with that.

In fact, this really opens the door for reparations for all. Wherever the government has committed an injustice, reparations will follow.

There were reports that many blacks were disenfranchised in Florida during the 2000 presidential election. They claimed they weren't allowed to vote. Okay, you get Disney World.

Everybody remembers the Rodney King beating caught on videotape in the early nineties. Unfortunately, many blacks have been beaten by the police in the past twenty years but weren't lucky enough to have had someone record it for posterity. All right, you guys get a camcorder. Have fun.

Many exclusive country clubs wouldn't allow black members until very recently. Let's see, you're already rich so you don't really need anything big. Okay, you get free range balls for a year, on any course. Hit 'em straight.

There are blacks with Indian blood but not enough to get a casino. All right, what happens in Vegas stays in Vegas, right? Okay, what happens wherever you are, stays right there.

Jena 6? You beat up a white boy and got away with it, you already got your reparations.

Colin Powell, the first black secretary of state, was embarrassed in front of the world when he made the case for war with faulty intelligence. Some feel he was duped by those with an Iraq agenda and reduced the most dignified brother in the world to a pathetic political lackey. Okay, any brother named Colin or Powell gets the Pentagon one weekend a month. Twice during black history month.

There are many brothers who live in areas, particularly in the South, that do not have black radio stations and are forced to listen to country music. Wow, um, hmmm, that's a tough one. I mean, it really kinda makes me laugh that you're forced to listen to country music. Okay, let me think about it, I'll get back to you guys.

Many blacks have been pulled over by police just for being black. This phenomenon is known as a DWB (driving while black). You get the 405 freeway in Los Angeles. No shooting at each other!

Some feel the low-income black areas have been unfairly targeted over the years with exploitative cigarette ads. Okay, any brother who smokes or has a bad cough, if you can find Tobacco Road, it's yours.

Wow, I'm still laughing at the brothers who have to listen to country music. Still haven't thought of a good reparation for you yet, so hang in there.

Any brother wrongly convicted of a crime in the last twenty-five years—and, by the by, wrongly does not mean somebody snitched. Wrongly means you didn't do it! Okay, you're pretty angry so you're going to need something good. I got it! One month out of every year, you get the Grand Canyon.

Believe it or not, the KKK is still known to pop their racists heads up now and then. Any brother hassled in any way by the KKK in the last twenty-five years gets free bed linens. Take my advice, get the high thread count.

Any brother in the armed forces who did something heroic overseas and then had to deal with a racist incident when they got back? Any racist incident. Sorry white people but the burden of proof is pretty low on this one. We are talking about decorated brothers. You guys get the use of three submarines. The only caveat is you have to use all three at the same time (national security reasons) and you have to take the country-music-listening brothers with you. See, I found something good for you guys.

Now some of you at this point may be saying, Hold on, Larry, can't we just apologize and call it a day? After all, we did apologize to the Japanese families who were detained in concentration camps. True, but you also gave them some cash and we've already established that's too impractical for us. Also, an apology allows us to move on and it's too much fun holding slavery over your heads instead of barreling into some closure.

Still others may be at the point of "Okay fine, we'll give you some money. What's it going to cost? Who cares, we'll pay whatever you want just please, give us back the Grand Canyon." You have no idea how tempted I am. But like I said earlier, it causes more problems than it solves.

At the end of the day, people need to know how bad the injustice perpetrated on black America really was. Money does something for us but nothing for you. But with my reparations you'll have a nice handy reminder with almost anything you do. Whether it's visiting the Black Grand Canyon or Black Disney World, driving the Black 405 or getting new sheets at Bed Bath Black and Beyond, you'll feel good knowing justice has been served.

You'll also learn a valuable lesson when it comes to righting societal wrongs. Pay your bill on time! Think of reparations like a parking ticket. If you had paid it on time (forty acres and a mule), you wouldn't have that big police boot on your tire. But it's very easy to get the boot off and start driving again.

Give us the Superdome.

Give Your Baby a "Nizame"

*W*ilmore has never really commented much on the hip-hop culture. When asked, he felt like he didn't quite understand and connect to it but had respect for the movement. In fact, one of the few times he discussed the topic was on his radio show when he interviewed the author of the book Give Your Baby a Nizame.

WILMORE: That's where I bought my Cadillac and you can too. Just ask for the friendly people at Mark Christoper. Tell them you heard this ad on *The Larry Wilmore Show.* (Show music.) Welcome back, everyone. I'm Larry Wilmore and you're listening to *The Larry Wilmore Show.* Today I am talking to hip-hop impresario Tiny P, author of the

new book called *Give Your Baby a Nizame.*
Welcome to the show, Tiny.

TINY P: What's up L dub? Shout-out to all my Tinies in
the P Pound.

WILMORE: Okay, shout-out noted. Tiny, tell us about
the book. What was the inspiration?

TINY P: No problem, Larry. I had just had my first kid.

WILMORE: Outside kid?

TINY P: No, inside. I was married.

WILMORE: You're kidding?

TINY P: Naw, come on, Larry. I'm gangsta on the
outside but on the inside I'm straight up Catholic.

WILMORE: You're Catholic?

TINY P: On the real. I was even an altar boy and shit.

WILMORE: Never thought I'd hear those words used
together.

TINY P: Sorry, Larry, I'm trying not to cuss.

WILMORE: I appreciate it. Of course, we are on delay so I'm able to take care of it. So you had a kid, and you were thinking of a name. Was this before the birth or after?

TINY P: Before. My wife and I were in that class where they got you breathin' and shi—sorry.

WILMORE: I caught it.

TINY P: Cool. Anyway, the teacher was all like inquirin' on people's baby names. And we was hearin' all these Jasons and Caitlins and Jessicas and Alexes and Ethans and were thinkin' damn, what kind of bullshit is this?

WILMORE: Caught it.

TINY P: You know what I'm saying? I didn't hear one name I would ever name my baby. How come people aren't giving their babies better names? Know what I'm saying?

WILMORE: So, you figured you would fill that need?

TINY P: Definitely. I've always been entrepreneurial and shit.

WILMORE: Caught it.

TINY P: So I decided to come up with this book.

WILMORE: That's great. So, you weren't happy with the more traditional American names going around and thought others might feel the same way?

TINY P: Exactly, exactly.

WILMORE: But aren't there a lot of African-American names out there?

TINY P: Yeah, but those aren't nizames, Larry. First, brothas put a "La" in front of a name and thought that was cool.

WILMORE: LaTonya, LaKeisha . . .

TINY P: Lasagna, all of those. Then they started namin' brothas after medicine and cars. Like Lexus, Corolla, Tylenol, Advil, or Levitra.

WILMORE: Levitra?

TINY P: I'm serious. I played basketball with a brotha named Purel.

WILMORE: That's the hand sanitizer.

TINY P: Exactly. And that nigga always had dirty hands. (He laughs.)

WILMORE: If I could get you not to use the "n" word, uh . . .

TINY P: No problem. My bad.

WILMORE: Okay, so not even current black names were appealing to you.

TINY P: Right. Except in the world of rap and hip-hop. That's where you find the best names, or nizames, today.

WILMORE: Well, they certainly are the most creative. We're going to take a break but when we come back I want to hear some of the nizames in your book. I also want to hear what you nizamed your baby. And we'll take some of your calls. You're listening to *The Larry Wilmore Show*. (Show music.)

WILMORE: Welcome back to *The Larry Wilmore Show*. Today's guest is Tiny P, hip-hop impresario and author of the book *Give Your Baby a Nizame*. Tiny, you were telling us what got you to the point where you felt this sort of book was needed. Before you continue, what is a nizame?

TINY P: A nizame is when you take part of a "normal" name and combine it with a character identifier about the person. It's a contraction of the words "nizzle" and "name."

WILMORE: Nizzle?

TINY P: Yeah, that's Snoop Speak for ni—

WILMORE: Black person, got it. So, a nizame is like a nickname?

TINY P: Naw, they're completely different. Let me break it down. Puff Daddy was a nickname for Sean "Puffy" Combs. But P. Diddy is his nizame.

WILMORE: I see. That makes sense. But now it's just Diddy, what does that mean?

TINY P: I don't know what the fuck that means. Sorry. Did you catch that?

WILMORE: Got it. Let's talk about the baby names.

TINY P: Nizames.

WILMORE: Nizames, right. Give me an example of some of the more popular nizames.

TINY P: No problem. You got DROOLY G, RUNNY D, COLIC E, and YDB to name a few.

WILMORE: YDB?

TINY P: YOUNG DIRTY BASTARD.

WILMORE: Of course. So they're kind of modeled after actual rapper names?

TINY P: Some are, some aren't. Sometimes it just takes one look at a dirty diaper and you know he's RUNNY D.

WILMORE: I guess that makes sense. I tell you what, let's take a call. Janice, you're on with Larry and Tiny P.

JANICE: Hey, Larry. What's up, TP?

TINY P: What's up?

JANICE: I'm expecting a girl next month.

WILMORE: Congratulations.

JANICE: Thank you. Any suggestions on girl nizames?

TINY P: Absolutely. You said you're having a lil' b?

JANICE: Uh, yes.

TINY P: How about LIL' B?

JANICE: Oh, that's cute. Thank you.

TINY P: Anytime.

WILMORE: The "B" stands for baby?

TINY P: Beotch.

WILMORE: Ouch. Isn't that kind of sexist?

TINY P: Yo, these are nizames, not names.

WILMORE: Okay, next caller. Chris, you're on with Tiny P.

CHRIS: Hey, Larry. Yo Tiny, I'm a big fan. I got your first CD *Ouija Board Homies*. It was dope.

TINY P: Righteous.

WILMORE: What's your question?

CHRIS: Check it out, brah, what if you and your wife can't agree on a name? Any suggestions?

WILMORE: Good question. How do you agree on a nizame?

TINY P: You want to really go with a nizame that expresses the essence of the kid. Once you get that, you'll probably agree. For example, let's say his actual name is William and he's sick a lot.

WILMORE: Let me guess, ILL WILL?

TINY P: Close, that's his nickname. His nizame would be ILL DUB.

WILMORE: Ahh, very good. I get it. So what if he isn't sick? What if he's just really calm?

TINY P: CHILL DUB.

WILMORE: Nice. Okay, what if he has asthma, he's easy-going, and his name is William?

TINY P: WEE Z DUB.

WILMORE: That is fucking awesome! Oh shit, now I gotta bleep myself.

TINY P: See, it's not so easy, is it?

WILMORE: What about time of year? Does the birth date itself have anything to do with the nizame?

TINY P: It can. Popular nizames for winter babies are all the LUDAS. You know, LUDACRIS, LU-DAMIC, LUDASUE, LUDALUKE, et cetera.

WILMORE: Okay, let's take one more call for Tiny P. Tonya, you're on with Larry and Tiny P.

TONYA: Thank you, Larry. I love your show.

WILMORE: Thank you.

TONYA: Tiny, my husband and I are adopting a Chinese girl. Is it appropriate to give her a nizame and if it is, do you have any suggestions?

TINY P: Hell yeah, it's appropriate. What's her given name?

TONYA: Susan.

TINY P: I would go with WU TANG ZU.

TONYA: That's fantastic, thank you.

TINY P: Good luck.

WILMORE: Tiny, I want to thank you for being my guest today. I think this is a fantastic service you're providing. And I love the whole idea of the nizame.

TINY P: Thanks, Larry, I appreciate it, and I hope everybody buys my book.

WILMORE: Oh wait, before we go, what did you name your daughter?

TINY P: Teeny P.

WILMORE: Lovely. I know she'll be proud of it. Coming up next is contrary hour. No matter what subject you bring up, I'll take the opposite point of view and destroy your argument. You're listening to *The Larry Wilmore Show*. (Show music.)

A Third Letter
to the NAACP

This is another one of Wilmore's attempts to get the civil rights group to adopt his revolutionary idea.

Dear Sir or Madam,

This is my follow up to my letter of three weeks ago. I haven't heard from you so I hope you got it. If not, I've attached it along with my original letter and my article. I won't bore you with the specifics in those again but I hope you got a chance to try out some of my "chocolate" ideas.

Speaking of ideas, I came up with what I think is a great way to spread it wide (that's what he said; sorry I couldn't resist).

Advertising!

That's right. Let's hire an advertising agency to blanket the media with the changeover. This could be fantastic. We could do like the Apple ads and have billboards that are completely blank with just the word "chocolate" in simple brown letters. People are going to look at it and say, "What the fuck?" (Excuse my French.)

And that's just the beginning. We could do different "chocolate" campaigns for different "chocolates." What are different "chocolates," you ask? Well, I'll tell you.

As you know, not all black people are 100 percent black. I'm talking both hue and heritage. We come in many different shades and combinations. These distinctions require specific "chocolate" designations. I've come up with a few, but believe me, there are many more.

Dark-Skinned Brothas = Dark Chocolate
This makes sense and is pretty self-explanatory.

Light-Skinned Brothas = Milk Chocolate
Since there is no "light" chocolate, milk chocolate will do. I fall into this category, by the way.

**Half-White, Half-Black Brothas =
Chocolate Milk**

This works because milk chocolate is merely a specific form of chocolate, whereas chocolate milk is the result of two things coming together to form a third.

Brothas Who Say They're Part French = Café Au Lait

Nuff said.

Fat Brothas = Chunky

A very popular old-school candy bar.

Rich or Uppity Brothas = $100,000 Bar

Another popular old-school candy bar.

Latinos Who Are Dark Enough to Look Black = Reese's Pieces

This works because technically they're more peanut butter than chocolate.

High Yellow Brothas = Caramel

This is a more specific form of light-skinned brotha.

Mixed Brothas (more than two races) = Whitman Sampler

This takes care of brothas like Tiger Woods.

White People Who Talk Black =
White Chocolate

This is already in circulation (Jason Williams of the Miami Heat) and replaces the very offensive yet accurate "wigger."

Mulatto = Mulatto

This is too good a name to change. Let's stick with it for a while.

Like I said, these are just a few ideas and suggestions. Please think them over, but we need to get on this ASAP! After an ad campaign we can start putting these terms in textbooks at schools. The possibilities are endless!

Looking forward to hearing from you soon.

Your Milk Chocolate Brotha,
Larry Wilmore
(Cell, voice mail only, 626-555-9894)
(chocolate5800612.pdf 135kb)
(letter8790011.pdf 28kb)
(letter8790012.pdf 28kb) attached

Text Messages from a Birmingham Jail

hough Wilmore was too young for the civil rights marches in the sixties, he was certainly inspired by the acts of civil disobedience the participants endured. He said he always admired Martin Luther King Jr.'s "Letter from Birmingham Jail" as the ultimate expression of an intelligent, oppressed voice making the case for equality and freedom. Wilmore also spent a night in a Birmingham jail, though it was not connected to any lofty undertaking. Nonetheless, he felt it a good opportunity for expression on an important topic.

WILMORE: I cnnot b leave im hear. seriously sum relly rasist cops. of corse, YMMV. times hv chngd n mos plces bt I guess nt her. :-(

OHLSON: were r u dude?

WILMORE: jail. brminghm AL

OHLSON: shit! LOL!

WILMORE: Not fnny. ths gys r sirius. like im bk in the 50s. so mch H8.

OHLSON: FWIW u shldnt b n AL n the 1st plays

WILMORE: OIC, u thnk this is funy?

OHLSON: ROTFL!! :'-D

WILMORE: W/E. u need 2 gt a lyf. p pul r hrtng. we ned chnge

OHLSON: k BOTOH sum p pul r doing ok.

WILMORE: IMHO we cn du bttr. F we jst got 2 no eech othr bttr it wld b gr8.

OHLSON: LBH, hus got tme?

WILMORE: u cn volntear :-)

OHLSON: BTDTGTTSAWIO!! _/!

WILMORE: JTLYK, vry sellfsh.

OHLSON: W/E. wen u gt out?

WILMORE: L8r 2 morow. :-<

OHLSON: RUOK?

WILMORE: TBH, i jst want my kds 2 hv a bttr lfe thn me. u no?

OHLSON: i no. ;-)

WILMORE: k, GTG. B4N.

OHLSON: L8R.

What's striking about this correspondence is Wilmore's sentimentality. You can really tell he just wants a better life for his kids.

KEY ———————————————————

YMMV:	your mileage may vary
LOL:	laugh out loud
H8:	hate
FWIW:	for what it's worth
OIC:	oh I see
ROTFL:	rolling on the floor laughing
:'-D:	crying laughing
W/E:	whatever
K:	okay
BOTOH:	but on the other hand
IMHO:	in my honest opinion
GR8:	great
LBH:	let's be honest
BTDTGTTSAWIO:	been there, done that, got the T-shirt, and wore it out
_/:	my glass is empty
JTLYK:	just to let you know
L8R:	later
RUOK:	are you okay?
TBH:	to be honest
GTG:	got to go
B4N:	bye for now

Bring Back the Shetland Negro

*W*ilmore always watched a lot of television and at one time thought about becoming a critic. In this essay, he offers a novel way to reinvigorate the black sitcom.

I'm a huge TV fan. Loved it ever since I was a kid. I can remember how proud I felt when I was young to see black stars on the tube. I had a crush on Diahann Carroll in *Julia*. I wanted to be as cool as Bill Cosby in *I Spy*. And I couldn't imagine anyone funnier than Flip Wilson from *The Flip Wilson Show*. I wasn't alone. All of America seemed to fall in love with these black pioneers of television as well as the ones to follow. Everybody said "dy-no-mite" in the seventies. We all wanted to be Huxtables in the eighties. And there's hardly one among us who can't recite *The Fresh Prince* theme song from the nineties.

Toward the end of that decade and into the new millennium the black sitcom has fallen on hard times. Many blame the decline of sitcoms in general for the fall-off but I don't think that's the reason. The problem is deeper than that. I think America has lost its connection to the black funny bone. It's not that America doesn't think black people are funny. On the contrary. Arguably, the most popular comedians of the past decade are Chris Rock and Dave Chappelle. And they are two very unapologetically "black" comedians.

I would suggest that Americans just don't feel comfortable laughing at black people anymore. It kinda makes sense. Ever since the O.J. trial, we've gone out of our way to call white people racist at every opportunity. And though we've had a lot of fun, they've gotten a bit gun shy. They want to laugh at black people but they don't want to be labeled racists. I believe I may have stumbled upon the perfect solution: Bring back the Shetland Negro.

The Shetland Negro (a term coined by comedian Tim Jones) is the diminutive Peter Pan–like brother who never gets big and makes everyone happy. Gary Coleman and Webster are the prime examples of this mutant phenomenon. They're always happy, real smart-alecky, walk funny, and fill people of all races with joy.

The first documented one burst on the scene in the early seventies when Rodney Allen Rippy was the teeny black spokesperson for Jack in the Box. The moment he uttered the phrase "it's too big a eat," America fell in love. And the affair was intense. Rippy was everywhere; award shows, talk shows, movie premieres, guest-star appearances, and more Jack in the Box commercials. It seemed as if this romance would never end. And then something strange happened. Rippy vanished.

Not all at once and not altogether. In fact, he didn't even go anywhere. It was something even more sinister. He started to grow. America was crushed. They had imagined this minuscule mandingo of mirth would be around to comfort them forever. Keep in mind, we had just endured Watergate, Vietnam, Nixon, and *The Mac Davis Show*. America was drained. They were grateful for the joy brought on by Rippy. But what were they supposed to do when he started getting older?

The rule of "once you go black, you never go back" is unfortunately canceled out by the rule "when black gets old, America turns cold." And let's be honest, once a little black kid stops being cute, he *really* stops being cute. It's like, once a leading lady loses her looks, she's a character actor, sorry. But we expect that from our sirens of the big screen. This took us by surprise. If America was a kid, somebody stole his pony.

Then a miracle happened. In an episode of the television show *Good Times* titled "Florida Gets a Job," a teeny sepia-toned tot sassed across the screen and into our hearts. His name: Gary Coleman.

To borrow a space-age metaphor, if Rippy was Sputnik, Coleman was the moon landing. America couldn't believe its good fortune. Not only was this licorice-flavored Lilliputian a laugh riot, he was guaranteed to stay little a long time. Gary suffered from a rare congenital kidney disease known as nephritis and consequently would never grow taller than forty-eight inches. Ironically, his malady released us from our malaise. America had found its Shetland Negro.

After *Good Times,* Coleman was seen again in various TV commercials and the show *The Jeffersons* before landing his big break as Arnold Jackson in the sitcom *Diff'rent Strokes.*

Now, if America thought it was in love before, it was head over heels beside itself when he uttered his famous catch phrase: "Whatchu talkin' bout, Willis?"

Diff'rent Strokes held out the fantasy that white people could actually adopt a Shetland of their own. This was too much for America to take and the show was an overnight smash. I can't tell you how many red-blooded Americans lived vicariously through Mr. Drummond.

After Coleman's meteoric rise, another Shetland came out of the stable. His name was Emmanuel Lewis and he played Webster on the TV show of the same name. Once again, a white couple adopts a Shetland Negro and everybody's happy. This Shetland's impact was so great that even to this day more people know him by his TV name, Webster, than by his actual name.

For a while, Shetlands were popping up all over the place to varying degrees of success but always embraced with affection. In fact, even a ventriloquist named Willie Tyler found unparalleled success on the comedy club circuit with his Shetland puppet, Lester. It may seem odd that a "fake" Shetland would find favor with the public but America didn't care. He was funny, black, and tiny, and as long as he stayed that way, they were happy.

Toward the end of the eighties and the beginning of the nineties, it seemed the Shetland couldn't get any more popular. Then a little bespectacled brotha with a big brain for comedy and a small pituitary for growing hit the scene. His name: Urkel.

With his catch phrase, "did I do that," this embryonic-sized ebony egghead stumbled across the soundstage and into our hearts. Damn, he was funny! Arguably the funniest of the Shetlands. But somewhere in about the fourth or fifth season, the unthinkable happened. That's right, he grew.

Whoa!

This was no Shetland at all. He was just a short, smart-alecky, late-blooming brotha. I mean, he grew a mustache on the show! What the hell?

America felt betrayed and the show didn't last much longer. Meanwhile, traces of the Shetland Negro could not be found anywhere.

It was just as well. The country needed some time to heal. And *Def Comedy Jam* was really funny! These black comedians weren't small but they really knew how to use the "f" word.

Occasionally, Gary Coleman would pop up on a TV show or in a commercial but no one seemed to care anymore. Even though he didn't grow, he did get old.

You see, a Shetland Negro's got about a fifteen- to twenty-year window of being cute. After that, they start showing their age and take on more of a pygmy vibe. That is not good. Even brothas are freaked out by pygmies. By the end of the nineties, it was clear that the era of the Shetland Negro was over. They had become extinct, if you will.

Now, just a few years later, the only evidence the Shetland even existed are the fossilized remains on TV Land. Look where we are. The sitcom is dead. The black sitcom is deader. And the terrorists are winning. Every time you turn on the tube, someone's getting shot, killed, or raped. And the terrorists are winning. Supposedly, reality shows have taken the place of comedies, only they're not funny and you have to check your brain at the door. And the terrorists are winning.

We need the Shetland Negro now more than ever!

So bring him back.

I guarantee you, America will be relieved to see an old friend. It would seem to me, in this post-9/11, endless-war world, America needs all the comfort food she can get.

So bring him back.

It can't be that hard to find one. Maybe there are some Shetland Negro farms we're not aware of that have thousands locked away like veal. Or maybe there's just one, sitting in his high chair at the kitchen table and sassing his relatives.

So bring him back.

Bring him back, mostly, because it's the right thing to do. The Shetland Negro is as American as baseball and hot dogs.

We need him now.

He's completely nonpartisan. He appeals to liberal largesse, conservative constraint, and black schadenfreude. He's never racist or sexist or homophobic. He doesn't mind fat people and he'll hang out with old geezers.

To put it plainly, he loves us and we love him.

So come back, little Negro, come back.

Random Black Thought #3

Don't Tase Me Bro!

If I'm a cop, and I'm a brotha, and they let me have a taser? Sorry bro, I'm tasing you.

A Fourth Letter to the NAACP

This is yet another attempt of Mr. Wilmore's to reach the NAACP.

Dir Sir or Madam,

Whew! What a couple of months. I have been so busy. You've probably been real busy too. I completely understand. There's a lot of racism out there and I bet you're up to your eyeballs in it. I'm sure my little proposal seems glaringly insignificant compared to a brotha getting a nasty look from a waitress at Denny's. That wasn't meant as sarcasm. I do believe brothas getting nasty looks from waitresses at Denny's is a huge problem. But I also believe that waitress would be giving a completely different look if she thought of that brotha as a tall cup of cocoa. By the way, do you have Jesse Jackson's cell number? I need to talk to him about something.

Anyhow, since I haven't heard from you, I've decided to take some matters into my own hands and I've got some really good news.

I got hip-hop!

That's right. I've convinced some of the biggest and up-and-coming rappers to incorporate the chocolate imagery into their songs. I really think you're going to love it and will see what I've been so passionate about in the last couple of letters I sent you but you haven't responded to yet. (That's not snarky. I know it's because you're busy.)

Anyhoo, check out some of these samples. (That's a joke.)

From the group BWJ (Brothas Without Jaws) comes a song about the yearnings for love. It's called "Lick My Choco-Pop."

Ridin' along in my Bentley
Comin' up to a stop
Bitches be gettin' all friendly
Puttin' up my convertible top

These hoes ain't gettin' in my pocket
This nigga don't haggle or shop
I just guide them down to the rocket
So they can lick my choco-pop

I realize it's a bit explicit but you have to admit it is catchy. It's even more so if you could hear the beat. Those guys are going to blow up real soon. They've already earned enough money to fix one of their jaws. And if we're smart, we can blow up "chocolate" right along with them.

I also have some calls in to Jay-Z, Diddy, Mos Def, Lil' Kim, Young Jeezy, and Lil Wayne. Actually, I've called all the Lil's and Youngs but so far I haven't heard back from anybody.

Well, that's all for now. I hope to hear from you soon.

I took the liberty of attaching the BWJ's song as a ringtone so you can get a better appreciation for it. Enjoy.

Your Milk Chocolate Brotha,
Larry Wilmore

P.S. It would be great if you could get me Jesse's number or his e-mail or his forwarding address. Thanks. Just send it to me in a text message.

(cell: 323-555-1280)

Please don't text any pics. :-)

(chocolate5800612.pdf 135kb)

(letter8790011.pdf 28kb)

(letter8790012.pdf 28kb)

(letter8790013.pdf 52kb)

(chocotone4005.mp3) attached

Angry Black Church Guide

*N*ot every angry black church is right for every brother. Some brothers just require a mild rebuke at society from the pulpit, while others need the motivating fuel of good old-fashioned black rage foaming out of the mouth of an equally upset black Jesus. While this may not seem like a big deal to some, look at all the trouble Barack Obama got in because of his angry black preacher. Most people weren't shocked by the tenor of Rev. Wright's rhetoric so much as the fact that Obama himself didn't appear to be that angry. In other words, he picked an angry black church that was a tad too peeved. If it had been revealed that Al Sharpton sat in those bitter pews for twenty years, no one would have blinked. Clearly we would have all agreed he made a compatible choice.

This is best expressed by Newton's Law (Huey P., not Isaac), which states that "the level of anger in a black church should be roughly equal to the level of anger in the brother attending said church." Recognizing this dilemma and how challenging it can be for blacks to choose the proper angry black church, Wilmore came up with a guide that cut through the chaff. The following are some excerpts.

1. MAD AS A MOFO METHODIST CHURCH OF MINNEAPOLIS/ST. PAUL

Double your anger, double your rage at this unapologetic temple of tantrums in the Twin Cities. This land of lakes landmark will keep your social life full while your spiritual life nurtures the narcotics of negativity. With its pitch-perfect blend of inaccurate history, conspiracy theory, and blaming whitey, Mad as a MoFo manages to get your blood hot but leaves your heart cold. And be sure to wear an extra layer of warmth during the winter of your discontent because Viking country is cold as a mofo when the days get short. Don't be put off by the lengthy three-hour tirades, MAAMF puts it all on CDs and DVDs so you can take your anger to go. Or download the diatribes directly onto MP3s. Now a high-tech lynching truly is high-tech. For the angry brother on the run, there's no better fit than Mad as a MoFo Methodist Church. Just don't run for office because this is the kind of shit that will definitely come back to haunt you.

RATING: 5 *Raised Black Fists*

2. OUR LADY OF HOSTILITY CATHOLIC CHURCH
   (BRISTOL, CONNECTICUT)

Though it's located in the same city as ESPN, there's nothing sporting about the racially charged accusations against the white man in this holiest of shrines. The architecture goes back a couple of centuries but the bad feelings go back even further, as "tradition" is the key word here. Hostility is not only in the name, it's in the decor, with its nineteenth-century style uncomfortable pews, confession stalls left over from the Inquisition, and a drab color scheme that says "we hate paint too." You'll appreciate the attention to detail in the Afrocentric stained-glass windows as black Jesus, black Mary, and the black Apostles make even hard brothers nervous with their never happy Ice Cube–like glares. And if you're non-Catholic, don't worry about completing the sacraments. The only confirmation they care about here is proof that the white man is evil. Attendance is not what it used to be, so you'll hear more Our Fathers than see our fathers, but racial tension in the air keeps it feeling full. Be sure to check out the Saturday Latin Mass, where racial finger pointing is doled out in mea maxima culpa style. With tithing at only 5 percent, Our Lady of Hostility is definitely good blame for your buck.

RATING: *3 Raised Black Fists*

3. BRISTLING BROTHERS BAPTIST CHURCH OF EAST ST. LOUIS

Located in a city famous for its ribs, these Bristling Brothers will definitely get in your grill when the subject is race. With its confrontational style, those looking for call and response will find their mouths full of foam from the rage being spewed in indiscriminate directions. And because the BBBC will blame anybody for racism, even whites can come in and find a home for their anger. But if you can't stand the heat don't pray in this kitchen, as old wounds can resurrect faster than Lazarus in this multiethnic melting pot congregation. Segregated softball games on Sundays put the icing on this blue-eyed devil's food cake. Recommended for those who like a little cream in their coffee but still like their coffee bitter.

RATING: *4 Raised Black Fists*

4. CHRIST THE LIGHT-SKINNED BROTHER CHURCH OF WASHINGTON, D.C.

Chocolate Jesus gives way to his caramel cousin in this mostly mulatto congregation. Sitting in the shadows of the nation's Capitol, these agitated children of God aren't shy about registering their votes on America's sins. Conservative dress and liberal use of the "n" word make for potent partisan partners of holy hate speech. For self-haters, there's a healthy dose of black-on-black blame to go around with the monthly "Where's your daddy?" series. And be sure to visit the Ebony and Ebony Bookstore where "What Would Black Jesus Do" wristbands and "Why Did Whitey Do" T-shirts are all the rage.

RATING: *4 Raised Black Fists*

5. FULL-BLOWN TEMPER OF CHRIST CHURCH OF SCOTTSDALE

The hot Arizona winds are no match for the heated bile spewing from this desert dome of demagoguery. Keeping with the cactus motif, "prickly" is the operative word here. Your eye will not see much friction but your ear will catch plenty of crazy made-up historical shit to keep you apoplectic for an eon. Started by a group of guilty white liberals, FBT of C spends just as much time apologizing as it does pointing the finger. And you'll want to give the finger to everyone after just five minutes of their award-winning sermons. Rated number one in incoherent rants in *Angry Black Church Annual*, its black ribbon stable of preachers constantly challenge any iota of reason left in your system. So if blind black rage is your destination then the Full-Blown Temper of Christ should be your first stop. When the desert sun gets too intense, remember it's not the heat, it's the white man.

RATING: *5 Raised Black Fists*

6. **SLIGHTLY PEEVED PENTECOSTAL CHURCH OF PALOS VERDES, CALIFORNIA**

Surf's up and so is your dander at this seaside California congregation—though you're more likely to catch a wave than a whiff of anger from these only slightly peeved Pentecostals. Breathtaking sunsets and beautiful vistas go a long way to make you forget ugly history. But what it lacks in intensity it makes up for in diversity, as speaking in tongues allows you to be rankled in long lost languages. Theater in the round seating is the perfect complement for its "circling around the issues" sermons. With its motto of "We're already loud so we don't need to be that angry," SPPC mostly uses its coastal setting to harbor boats instead of resentments. With just enough ire to stir the pot but with the burners on simmer, Slightly Peeved Pentecostal Church could be the perfect fit for the brother not ready to let go of his anger but in no hurry to dish it out either. For you out-of-towners, be sure to get the map to racist stars' homes in the bookstore.

RATING: *2 Raised Black Fists*

7. GOSPELS AND GRUDGES UNITY CHURCH OF PHILADELPHIA

The City of Brotherly Love dishes out equal portions of God and grumble in this historic institution. They won't ask you to declare independence from the Man but you better have a good constitution for the three-hour-plus sermons. With an Afrocentric point of view as cracked as the Liberty Bell, G and G pretty much paints everybody in the Bible with the same black brush. Some sample "proving" lectures include: "Why Moses Was Black" ("They wandered in the desert for forty years. You know brothers hate asking for directions"), "Why David Was Black" ("Who else would have a girlfriend named Bathsheba?"), and "Why Job and Jonah Were Not Black" ("First of all, no brother's got that much patience, and second, no brother's going to get close enough to a whale to get eaten by it"). The most entertaining of the conspiracy temples, Gospels and Grudges Unity Church is a rollicking refuge of revolutionary rhetoric but not even Thomas Paine could find any common sense.

RATING: *3 Raised Black Fists*

Fair Trial

a fter delivering the eulogy for the "n" word, Wilmore realized it was symbolically executed without really receiving a fair trial. He had the word symbolically exhumed and then proceeded with the hearing. The following are some of the highlights of the court transcripts as well a dose of my personal observations.

The mood in the courtroom was electric with anticipation. No one thought Wilmore would have the "n" word exhumed, let alone bring it to trial. The gallery was packed with journalists, along with a few celebrities and even some paparazzi.

Wilmore looked confident at the defendant's table, while the prosecution seemed a bit reserved. The jury was a mix of ethnicities, with the men slightly outnumbering the women. Judge Brightman entered the courtroom, everyone stood, and the trial began. The prosecution went first.

DISTRICT ATTORNEY: Ladies and gentlemen of the jury, Your Honor, distinguished guests, we are here today to do something that many of us thought was already done. The banishment of a word so vile that we can refer to only its first letter, "n." This word is hateful, divisive, cruel, and has no place in our modern societal vocabulary. The defense will try to get you to believe we should ignore this legacy. Act as if this word isn't really all that bad and should be left alone. Well, maybe while we're at it, we should let murderers go free too. After all, a lot of people kill, so it can't be all that bad. And we may as well free all the rapists and child molesters and arsonists and burglars and terrorists and anyone else guilty of inflicting irreparable harm upon society. I apologize for sounding rather flip, but I can't help but scoff at even the mention of something so outrageous. We will prove today that this horrible word should be put back into the ground where it belongs so it can wither and decay until there's nothing left. And as far as I'm concerned, the faster it decomposes, the quicker we can heal. Thank you.

Pretty strong opening remarks from the D.A. Everyone seemed pretty impressed. It felt like everyone was on the same page, and at this point it seemed unlikely that Wilmore would be able to garner any sympathy. He got up very confidently but with a serious and stern look on his face.

WILMORE: Ladies and gentlemen of the jury, Your Honor, distinguished guests, anyone I've left out, why are we here today? No, seriously, why are we here? No, really, why? No, seriously, I want to know, because this all seems a little suspicious to me. Of all the offensive words in the English language that we could choose to ban, we pick on the one black people use the most? Good lookin' out bro.

The gallery laughed. Wilmore continued.

WILMORE: Seriously though, no one else finds it strange that only the "n" word is getting picked on? Last time I checked, that was called racial profiling. And the time I checked before that, racial profiling was wrong. But the prosecution is going to try and convince you that what you're doing is necessary. Really? Is it really necessary? The prosecution has admitted in his opening remarks that at the present time it can be referred to only by its first letter, which means we've already discarded "igger." So now he's saying we have to get rid of the letter "n" too? Really? The letter "n" is so upsetting that we have to kill it? You know, my crazy uncle is upsetting, but I don't think he should be executed. After this trial, I think you will agree with me, ladies and gentlemen of the jury, that this is a whole lot of nothing. I'm sorry, the letter "n" is evil. A whole lot of othing.

Wilmore sits down to some laughter. The D.A. did not look pleased and it was hard to read the jury. After some courtroom formalities, the prosecution called its first witness.

DISTRICT ATTORNEY: Could you please state your name and what you do.

WITNESS: My name is Professor Lester Rivers. I teach sociology at the University of California at Irvine.

DISTRICT ATTORNEY: Professor Rivers, are you familiar with the "n" word?

PROFESSOR RIVERS: Yes, I am.

DISTRICT ATTORNEY: How did the word originate?

PROFESSOR RIVERS: Many feel it was sometime in the middle of the eighteenth century, during the American slave trade, when blacks from Africa were first referred to as Nigers, after the country. Over the years the slave masters, partly through their hatred of blacks and partly through bad English, adopted the more pejorative and hateful word that is on trial today.

DISTRICT ATTORNEY: Was this word ever used in a positive context?

PROFESSOR RIVERS: Oh no. It was always meant as a way to dehumanize and humiliate.

DISTRICT ATTORNEY: Is it still used that way?

PROFESSOR RIVERS: I believe so.

DISTRICT ATTORNEY: Is that your professional opinion or your personal one?

PROFESSOR RIVERS: Both. I think no matter how you dress it up, it still carries the scars of the originally intended insult.

DISTRICT ATTORNEY: Thank you. Your witness.

The D.A. sat down and looked pleased. Wilmore rose and addressed the professor.

WILMORE: Professor Rivers, you say you're familiar with the "n" word?

PROFESSOR RIVERS: That's correct.

WILMORE: Good. Could you point one out for me in the courtroom, please?

DISTRICT ATTORNEY: I object! Your Honor, that is inappropriate.

JUDGE BRIGHTMAN: Mr. Wilmore, you will refrain from this type of questioning. Objection sustained.

WILMORE: Yes, Your Honor.

Wilmore took a moment to regroup.

WILMORE: Professor, are you married?

PROFESSOR RIVERS: Yes, I am.

WILMORE: Long time?

PROFESSOR RIVERS: Twenty-two years.

WILMORE: Congratulations. Would you say you have a typical relationship with your wife?

DISTRICT ATTORNEY: I object. Your Honor, the professor's personal life is not on trial here.

JUDGE BRIGHTMAN: Mr. Wilmore, what is the point of this line of inquiry?

WILMORE: I'm getting to it right now, Your Honor. Your relationship with your wife could be described as typical, wouldn't you say?

PROFESSOR RIVERS: I suppose.

WILMORE: Let me be a little clearer. For instance, I bet like most wives, she probably gets on you a lot to do certain things.

PROFESSOR RIVERS: Well, yeah, I guess. I mean, we've been married twenty-two years.

The courtroom laughed.

WILMORE: Exactly. I've been married fourteen years and my wife nags me all the time to clean up the garage. Has your wife ever nagged you, Professor?

DISTRICT ATTORNEY: I object! Your Honor, please.

JUDGE BRIGHTMAN: Mr. Wilmore, this better go somewhere or I'm going to have to stop this entire line of questioning.

WILMORE: Coming right up, Your Honor. Professor, has your wife ever nagged you? Keep in mind, you're under oath.

PROFESSOR RIVERS: Well, yes.

WILMORE: Your wife has nagged you. Interesting. One who nags would be called what, Professor?

PROFESSOR RIVERS: I'm sorry?

WILMORE: One who nags, Professor, what is the name for that? Let me help you out. One who bags is a bagger. One who tags is a tagger. Now, one who nags would be a . . . ?

DISTRICT ATTORNEY: I object! Your Honor, this has nothing to do with anything.

WILMORE: Your Honor, I'm trying to establish a correlation between commonly used words and the defendant, who, in case we've all forgotten, is a word.

JUDGE BRIGHTMAN: I'll allow it. Objection overruled. Answer the question, Professor.

WILMORE: One who nags is . . . ?

PROFESSOR RIVERS: A nagger.

WILMORE: I'm sorry, I couldn't hear you. Could you repeat it again, a little louder?

PROFESSOR RIVERS: A nagger.

WILMORE: Wow. A nagger. We both are married to naggers. Do you realize our wives are the letter "i" away from being something so bad we'd have to kill it? Do you think that's fair to the ninth letter of the alphabet?

PROFESSOR RIVERS: I don't know.

WILMORE: You don't know. You don't know. But you do know you're in love with a nagger?

DISTRICT ATTORNEY: Your Honor—

JUDGE BRIGHTMAN: Mr. Wilmore—

WILMORE: That's all.

The professor left the witness stand looking a bit confused. It's tough to say who was winning at that point.

The D.A. presented his next several witnesses. They were a couple of cultural pundits and a black clergyman. He pretty much stuck to his straightforward approach of attacking the historical impact of the word and its incendiary uses. Wilmore's cross-examinations continued to focus on semantics and to portray the "n" word as a victim of discrimination.

The prosecution then called its final witness. He was an older black gentleman who seemed to have his difficult life story etched on his distinguished weathered face.

DISTRICT ATTORNEY: Could you please state your name and what you do?

WITNESS: My name is William Graves and I'm retired. Before that, I ran my own business. I started off shining shoes at Union Station and eventually I started selling shoe accessories.

DISTRICT ATTORNEY: Where did you grow up?

GRAVES: I'm from Mississippi, the deep South.

DISTRICT ATTORNEY: How old are you, Mr. Graves?

GRAVES: Ninety-two years young and still have an eye for the ladies.

DISTRICT ATTORNEY: I'm sure you do. Would it be fair to say you've seen your share of racism in your day?

GRAVES: Yes sir, I'd say it'd be very fair.

There was a bit of laughter from the crowd. More out of respect than anything else.

DISTRICT ATTORNEY: Have you ever been called the "n" word?

GRAVES: You're kidding, right?

Once again the gallery laughed.

DISTRICT ATTORNEY: Would you be so kind as to share one of these unfortunate incidents with the jury?

GRAVES: Sure will. I was on an all-black junior base-ball team when I was a kid and one year we had the best team in the state. Personally, I thought we were the best in the whole damn country, but that's my opinion. Anyhow, back then you couldn't be black and be better than the white teams. See, we had to play in an all-black league but because we were so good we qualified for the state tourney. The parents of the other teams threatened to not show up at all if our team was allowed to compete. Because I grew up in the

South, I knew about racism but that was the first time it really affected me personally. But I still couldn't understand it. Then I was watching television and they were interviewing one of the parents. And he said—

Mr. Graves paused here. It seemed the emotions of recalling that event really took over him.

DISTRICT ATTORNEY: Take your time, Mr. Graves. What did the man say on television?

MR. GRAVES: He said, "There's no way I'm gonna let my boy play ball with a bunch of niggers." I never forgot that.

DISTRICT ATTORNEY: I can understand why. Thank you, Mr. Graves. Your witness.

WILMORE: No questions, Your Honor. Thank you, Mr. Graves.

To say that was very powerful is to grossly understate it. The gallery hung on every one of Graves's words. On this high note, the prosecution rested.

After a break for lunch, Wilmore called his first witness.

WILMORE: Could you state your name and what you do, please?

WITNESS: Yo, my name is Painful P and I'm in the hip-hop group S.T.D.

WILMORE: Mr. P, would you describe yourself as very successful?

PAINFUL P: I would describe myself as a brotha who got over on a mothafucka, if that's what you mean.

JUDGE BRIGHTMAN: Counsel, would you please advise the witness to curtail his language.

WILMORE: Actually, Your Honor, his language is a very important part of his testimony.

JUDGE BRIGHTMAN: All right, but just watch it.

WILMORE: You bet. Mr. P, before you "got over," what was your life like?

PAINFUL P: Shit, I did whatever a nigga had to do, know what I'm sayin'? Hustlin', pimpin' whatever, know what I'm sayin'?

WILMORE: I believe I have an idea. You were broke and did all you could to make ends meet. So what changed all that?

PAINFUL P: My first CD. It went platinum and you know, a nigga had arrived.

WILMORE: What was the name of the CD?

PAINFUL P: The Nigga Has Arrived.

The gallery laughed.

WILMORE: So if not for the "n" word, you might still be in the ghetto hustlin' and pimpin'?

PAINFUL P: No doubt. Shit, I'd probably be dead, know what I'm sayin'?

WILMORE: Yes, I do. You're saying the "n" word saved your life.

DISTRICT ATTORNEY: I object! He's putting words in his mouth.

WILMORE: No more questions.

The district attorney cross-examined but didn't get much. Wilmore then called his next witness.

WILMORE: Could you please state your name and what you do?

WITNESS: My name is Jeffrey the Articulater. I'm a comedian.

WILMORE: Could you describe your style of comedy?

THE ARTICULATER: Sure. I articulate the truth.

WILMORE: Articulate the truth, could you elaborate?

THE ARTICULATER: I point out the differences between people, mainly white people and black people. You know, like, white people do blah blah blah but niggas be doin' blah blah blah.

WILMORE: Blah blah blah being the subject of the joke?

THE ARTICULATER: Correct.

WILMORE: Couldn't you just say white people do blah blah blah but black people do blah blah blah?

THE ARTICULATER: I could but "niggas" is funnier.

The gallery laughed.

THE ARTICULATER: See?

WILMORE: I do. But Mr. The Articulater, isn't it offensive to call black people niggas?

THE ARTICULATER: I'm not calling black people niggas. I'm making a distinction between black and white and using "niggas" as the representation of a certain type of black person. And it's the recognition of that representation that elicits laughter from the audience.

WILMORE: Very well articulated.

THE ARTICULATER: Thank you.

WILMORE: No further questions.

The D.A. did his best to try and discredit the witness on cross but he was just too damn articulate. After a short break, Wilmore called his last witness, which turned out to be quite a surprise to everyone, including the witness.

WILMORE: I would now like to call Mr. William
    Graves to the stand.

DISTRICT ATTORNEY: Your Honor, I object. Mr.
    Graves is not on the witness list.

JUDGE BRIGHTMAN: Mr. Wilmore?

WILMORE: That's correct, Your Honor, but some
    new evidence has come to my attention, evidence
    that can be corroborated only by Mr. Graves.
    And besides, we're not in court for a traffic ticket.
    My client's life is on the line.

JUDGE BRIGHTMAN: All right, I'll allow it. Objection
    overruled.

William Graves walked back up to the stand, where just
hours before he had everyone close to tears with his
heartfelt story.

WILMORE: Mr. Graves, first of all I want to thank you
    for your brave testimony earlier.

MR. GRAVES: Just telling it how I see it.

WILMORE: And I appreciate that. Mr. Graves, do you
   see the man sitting in the back of the gallery with
   the red cap on?

MR. GRAVES: Red cap . . . My vision's not so good.

WILMORE: Take a good look.

MR. GRAVES: Oh yes, I see a gentleman with a
   red cap—Oh my god. Don't tell me, no.

WILMORE: You recognize him, don't you?

MR. GRAVES: Is that Tommy Knuckleball Kinnebrew?

WILMORE: I believe it is.

The man with the red cap waved to Mr. Graves, who
waved back. There was a bit of murmur in the courtroom
as it seemed no one knew where Wilmore was going.

MR. GRAVES: I haven't seen you in sixty years.

The man in the red cap nodded and smiled.

WILMORE: Could you explain to the courtroom your
   relationship with Mr. Kinnebrew?

MR. GRAVES: Tommy and I played ball together, all through school. We were the best of friends. We lost touch after I went into the navy.

WILMORE: So Mr. Kinnebrew was your closest friend in the whole world.

MR. GRAVES: That's right. We went through some times. Look at you, you old dog, you haven't changed a bit.

WILMORE: Old dog, was that his nickname?

MR. GRAVES: No, his nickname was Red, cause he had red hair. We also called him Knuckleball because he had the best knuckleball in the league.

WILMORE: Those are the nicknames that everyone called him. You had your own personal nickname as well, didn't you?

DISTRICT ATTORNEY: I object! This is irrelevant.

JUDGE BRIGHTMAN: Counsel, this walk down memory lane, though pleasant, is hardly serving the best interests of the court. Please make your point.

WILMORE: I will, Your Honor. Answer the question,
Mr. Graves. Did you have your own personal
nickname for Mr. Kinnebrew?

MR. GRAVES: I don't understand.

WILMORE: What's to understand, Mr. Graves? Did you
have a personal nickname for Mr. Kinnebrew or
didn't you?

MR. GRAVES: I don't remember.

WILMORE: You don't remember. Well let me help
you jog your memory. When you first saw
Mr. Kinnebrew, what did you want to say?

MR. GRAVES: I—uh—

He seemed to be struggling. No one was quite sure what
was going on.

WILMORE: Say it, Mr. Graves. Say what you wanted
to say when you saw Mr. Kinnebrew. What you
always said when you saw Mr. Kinnebrew. What
you would've said had we all not been in here and
you were not a witness for the prosecution. Say it!

MR. GRAVES: That's my nigga.

WILMORE: I'm sorry, what did you say?

MR. GRAVES: That's my nigga!

The gallery was hushed, quite shocked by this revelation.

WILMORE: (shaking his head) That's your nigga. Isn't that something? The man who has experienced more racism than arguably anyone here, the man who was scarred by the defendant, uses the defendant as a term of endearment. Your Honor, if this is not proof of my client's innocence, then there is no such thing as justice. The defense rests.

The gallery erupted in spontaneous applause. Wilmore really seemed to make his case. After closing arguments from both sides, the jury retired to deliberate. They were away for only two hours and came back with a verdict. Guilty. The "n" word was symbolically executed once more and ordered back into the ground.

Wilmore was very upset and never practiced law again.

Sudoku

I have no black thoughts on sudoku.

The Last Letter to the NAACP

I believe this was Wilmore's last letter to the
civil rights group trying to convince them to
change "African-American" to "chocolate."

My Chocolate Brotha or Sista,
For some reason, we keep missing each other. Or
maybe you never got my other letters. Or maybe
I have the wrong address and some stranger is
reading this. If that's the case, I hope you're
"chocolate," Mr. Stranger. And I hope you've
taken some of my suggestions. If I do have the
address and you're simply not responding to me,
I don't know what to say. To pretend that my

feelings aren't hurt would be misleading. But I'm not writing you to expound on my bruised ego. That would be rude. As rude as, say, not responding to repeated correspondences on an extremely important matter!

Sorry, I got a little carried away. I'm just trying to understand you. You know what, you take the credit. I don't need it. Yeah, I came up with "chocolate," yeah, it could make me immortal, yeah, I could probably get laid more, but you take it. If that's what's holding you up, then please, take all the credit.

Is it money? I know I haven't given you any donations since the nineties, is that it? Look, I'm sorry. My budget's been tight. But if money is the only thing coming between us, then I'll write you a check right now!

If it's not money and it's not the credit, then I can only assume I haven't sucked up enough to you guys. I can't believe I would make such a stupid mistake. Not that you would want me to stoop that low, a classy organization such as yourself. By the way, on a side note, I love what you guys have done with the Image Awards. I watched it in HD and it fucking rocked! (Excuse my French.) It really should be a live show.

I'm sure if brothas weren't so unpredictable, it would be.

Um, I really really really really really think you should consider this. Really. Seriously. I'm not going to beg you, but pleeeeeeeeeeeeeease, think about it.

By the way, your participation will be greeted with the utmost respect and will be given serious consideration.

How do I know this? Because I feel it in my heart. I wouldn't be writing this in my underwear right now if I didn't feel it in my heart.

Come on. Do it. Do it. Do it. Do it. Do it. Do it. Do it. Do it. Do it.

You know you want to.

Do you guys not like chocolate? Is that the deal? Have some Ghirardelli milk chocolate caramel squares and then talk to me. Or just talk to me.

Okay, fine. I get it. The National Association for the Advancement of Chocolate People doesn't want to admit who they are (or is it who it is?).

Don't worry about it. You stay in that twentieth century of yours. I'll be blazing the way to the twenty-first and beyond. And just for the record, I've never sent you any money.

Have a good life.

Your Milk Chocolate Brotha Who You Won't
Recognize,
Larry Wilmore

P.S. I sent you a request to be my friend on
Facebook and you haven't confirmed it yet.
So if you could . . .

We're not sure if the NAACP ever responded to Wilmore
and Facebook shows no record of them ever becoming
friends.

How Come Brothas Don't See UFOs? PART II

a bout a year after Wilmore opined on the non-
existence of brothas and UFO sightings, he released
this fascinating interview.

Last year I reported my dissatisfaction with the lack of
reported brotha UFO incidents. I gave many theories (all
of which I believe could be true) and ended with the
thought of a possible government cover-up. I felt, how
could there not even be one brotha who'd seen a UFO in
the sixty years they've been reported?

Since that time, I've made a fascinating discovery.
Project Blue Book, the top-secret program created to
collect UFO data, apparently had an "above" top-secret

drawer called Project Black Book. Black Book documented at least thirty-odd cases of close encounters of the black kind. The majority of those cases, unfortunately, seemed explainable. They could be dismissed as either one or a combination of factors, like natural phenomena, secret military craft, less than credible character, and psychiatric issues. A few, however, seemed to defy these odds and were given a special status called Black Hole.

Apparently, these particular sightings were to be "buried" so deeply that it would seem they had gone into a black hole. I find this extremely fascinating. The government always seemed concerned about UFO reports but seemed especially paranoid about "black" UFO reports. Maybe they were afraid disaffected blacks would team up with aliens to take over. As far-fetched as this sounds, remember how poorly brothas were treated back then. The government was already frightened that angry groups like the Black Panthers were arming themselves with guns. But brotha anger combined with alien technology?! It's hard not to see their point.

I thought I would investigate the Black Hole people myself. Unfortunately, two have already passed away and the other, a Mr. Bev Williams, refused my request. But after persistent follow-ups and assurances of my credibility, Mr. Williams granted an interview. The following is the transcript of that visit.

Wilmore session with Mr. Bev Williams: recorded 2/17/03

WILMORE: Could you state your name for me please, sir?

MR. WILLIAMS: My name is Beverly Williams.

WILMORE: Your name is Beverly?

MR. WILLIAMS: Yes sir, yes it is.

WILMORE: Wow. I mean, I knew it was Bev but I didn't realize it was short for Beverly.

MR. WILLIAMS: That's my name.

WILMORE: Was it a common pratice when you were young to give guys girls' names?

MR. WILLIAMS: It's not just a girl's name. It was a very popular boy's name at the time.

WILMORE: Really? I don't recall any famous men named Beverly. There's Frankie Beverly but that's his last name.

MR. WILLIAMS: Did you come here to make fun of my name?

WILMORE: No, no, no, I'm sorry, I want to ask you some questions about the evening of August third, 1956. Can you tell us what happened?

MR. WILLIAMS: That was a long time ago. I can barely remember what I had for breakfast today.

WILMORE: Remember what we talked about on the phone? The UFO?

MR. WILLIAMS: Oh yeah, the ship, sure I remember. Yes, I did see one.

WILMORE: Okay, can you be a little more specific? Give us a few details?

MR. WILLIAMS: Sorry, I know I saw something but I don't know much more beyond that. It's uh, it's kinda cloudy.

WILMORE: I understand, I understand. Mr. Williams, it appears the government may have buried the memory of your experience deep in your cerbral cortex. I hope you don't mind, but I've brought with me a doctor who's going to help you to understand and recall what happened that night. Is that okay?

MR. WILLIAMS: I suppose.

WILMORE: Dr. Quinones?

DR. QUINONES: Mr. Williams, I'm a psychologist who specializes in regressive hypnosis. I'm going to put you into a state of deep relaxation that will resemble sleep but you will be totally aware of your surroundings and everything I say. Do you understand?

MR. WILLIAMS: I do.

After ten minutes of inducing Mr. Williams, Dr. Quinones continues.

DR. QUINONES: Mr. Williams, can you hear me?

MR. WILLIAMS: Yes, I can hear you.

DR. QUINONES: I want you to go to a place in your memory that's been locked away for a long time. A place that seems impossible to get inside. Imagine yourself standing outside of that place right now. Tell me what you see.

MR. WILLIAMS: I see a door.

DR. QUINONES: Good. I want you to open that door.

MR. WILLIAMS: I can't. It's locked.

DR. QUINONES: That's great. That locked door represents his repressed memory.

WILMORE: Wow. Get him to open it.

DR. QUINONES: Mr. Williams, I want you to look to the right of the door. Do you see the key hanging on the wall?

MR. WILLIAMS: To the right? Yes, yes, I do see a key.

DR. QUINONES: Good. Take that key and use it to unlock the door. Do it now.

MR. WILLIAMS: Okay.

WILMORE: This is so effing awesome.

MR. WILLIAMS: There, I did it. I unlocked it. It wouldn't turn at first but then I put my weight on it and then it moved. I've always found that if you get leverage on a lock you can always—

DR. QUINONES: Yes, yes, Mr. Williams, that's fine.

WILMORE: Tell him to go inside.

DR. QUINONES: Mr. Williams, I want you to walk inside that door. I want you to do that right now.

MR. WILLIAMS: Okay. Should I take the key with me?

DR. QUINONES: Uh, sure.

MR. WILLIAMS: But what if somebody needs it? Maybe I should put it back.

DR. QUINONES: That's fine.

MR. WILLIAMS: On the other hand, I don't want anybody following me in here. What if they have a knife?

WILMORE: Tell him just to leave the damn key and walk through the door.

DR. QUINONES: Mr. Williams, do whatever makes you feel comfortable. Now, I want you to describe what you see.

MR. WILLIAMS: Okay. I think I'm on the side of a large hill or mountain.

WILMORE: Great. I think this is it.

DR. QUINONES: Tell me more about that mountain.

MR. WILLIAMS: I feel tired. Like I've been running, climbing.

DR. QUINONES: Yes, yes, go on.

MR. WILLIAMS: Bright lights, up in the sky, circling.

WILMORE: UFOs?

DR. QUINONES: Describe them.

MR. WILLIAMS: Large, bubble-shaped front with a long cigar-shaped back and long protruding blades on top circling very fast.

WILMORE: That sounds like a helicopter.

MR. WILLIAMS: Yes, helicopter.

WILMORE: What else? We need more.

DR. QUINONES: Are these helicopters after you?

MR. WILLIAMS: Not sure. I just know I must get to the place.

WILMORE: What place?

DR. QUINONES: What place, Mr. Williams?

MR. WILLIAMS: I'm not sure. But I must go.

DR. QUINONES: Do you feel compelled to go there?

MR. WILLIAMS: Yes, compelled.

DR. QUINONES: As if some force is pulling you?

MR. WILLIAMS: Yes, some force. She feels it too.

DR. QUINONES: She?

MR. WILLIAMS: Yes, the white lady with me. They took her son and she started drawing pictures of this mountain but didn't know why.

WILMORE: That sounds familiar. Ask him if he sculpted the mountain out of mashed potatoes.

DR. QUINONES: Did you sculpt the mountain out of mashed potatoes?

MR. WILLIAMS: Yes, mashed potatoes. And one half of my face got burned and my wife got mad.

WILMORE: That's *Close Encounters of the Third Kind.* He's remembering a movie.

DR. QUINONES: Mr. Williams, I think we are inside of a false memory. A block of some sort. I want you to look for another door.

MR. WILLIAMS: That's a big-ass mothership.

DR. QUINONES: Focus, Mr. Williams. Do you see another door?

MR. WILLIAMS: Yes, I do. It's on the side of the hill.

DR. QUINONES: Good. That door represents where his actual memory is buried. The false memory of the movie was preventing him from accessing it.

WILMORE: Brilliant.

DR. QUINONES: Mr. Williams, I want you to unlock this door and walk through it.

MR. WILLIAMS: Okay. There's no key. I kept the one from the other door, should I use that?

DR. QUINONES: Sure, use that.

MR. WILLIAMS: It worked.

DR. QUINONES: Great, now walk through.

MR. WILLIAMS: Should I ask the white lady if she wants to come too?

DR. QUINONES: Uh—

WILMORE: Tell him to leave the white lady. She's busy being in a movie.

DR. QUINONES: I want you to go in by yourself.

MR. WILLIAMS: Okay. Good luck finding your son.

DR. QUINONES: Look around, Mr. Williams.
　　Tell me what you see.

MR. WILLIAMS: Everything's shiny, clean, lots of
　　buttons and panels, very futuristic-looking.

WILMORE: He could be on an alien ship.
　　Ask him to describe it.

DR. QUINONES: Be a little more specific, Mr. Williams.

MR. WILLIAMS: I feel like I have no weight.
　　Like I can float.

WILMORE: Oh shit. Maybe they took him into space.
　　Is he in space?

DR. QUINONES: Are you in space?

MR. WILLIAMS: Yes, I believe so. Yes, definitely.

WILMORE: Does he know where? Is he near Earth or
　　did they take him to their home planet?

DR. QUINONES: Are you above Earth?

MR. WILLIAMS: I don't think so. Not sure where we are.

WILMORE: We? Ask him to describe the others.

DR. QUINONES: What do the others look like?
Are they humanoid?

MR. WILLIAMS: I think so. They have shiny skin.

WILMORE: Wow. I think this is it. Have him ask them
who they are and what they want.

DR. QUINONES: Mr. Williams, I want you to ask them
who they are and what they want.

MR. WILLIAMS: Okay. Who are you and what do you
want? Really? No, I'm sorry, I don't.

WILMORE: What did they say?

DR. QUINONES: What did they say?

MR. WILLIAMS: They said they are a family like the
one I come from. Then they asked me if I knew
how to get to Earth. I said I didn't.

WILMORE: How to get to Earth? They abducted him. Why would they ask him that?

DR. QUINONES: Why did they ask you that?

MR. WILLIAMS: They said they were lost.

WILMORE: Lost? *Lost in Space*? That's a TV show! Come on, Doctor!

MR. WILLIAMS: They said Dr. Smith sabotaged their navi-computer.

WILMORE: Doctor, what is going on? He keeps referencing fiction.

DR. QUINONES: Apparently, whoever buried his memory did a very good job of keeping it inaccessible.

WILMORE: Is there any way we can access it?

DR. QUINONES: It's possible. But risky.

WILMORE: Why?

DR. QUINONES: Because I access the most sensitive part of the memory. If you're not careful, the person could have a nervous breakdown.

MR. WILLIAMS: Home. He needs to phone home.

WILMORE: Shut up, that's *E.T.* I think we're too late for that, Doc. You may as well give it a try.

DR. QUINONES: Very well. But I warn you, if it gets too intense, I'm taking him out.

WILMORE: Of course.

DR. QUINONES: Mr. Williams, I want you to look for another door. Do you see it?

MR. WILLIAMS: Yes. Do you want me to go in?

DR. QUINONES: No. I want you to look to the left of that door. Look at the floor. Do you see a hatch?

MR. WILLIAMS: Yes.

DR. QUINONES: I want you to open that hatch and climb down.

WILMORE: This better not fucking be *Lost*.

MR. WILLIAMS: I'm scared.

DR. QUINONES: I know. But it's okay. Just lower yourself down.

MR. WILLIAMS: Okay. It's dark.

DR. QUINONES: Lower yourself down the ladder. Tell me when you've reached the bottom.

MR. WILLIAMS: I got my eyes closed. Okay, I'm at the bottom.

DR. QUINONES: Great. Open your eyes.

MR. WILLIAMS: Okay. No! Don't! Don't do that to him!

DR. QUINONES: What's going on? Don't do what?

MR. WILLIAMS: They're cutting him open. Stop!

WILMORE: Cutting who open?

DR. QUINONES: What's happening, Mr. Williams?

MR. WILLIAMS: My name is Beverly Williams, I'm a
   janitor at a top-secret government installation
   called Area 51. I have witnessed secret government
   aircraft being tested as well as actual alien craft.
   Recently they recovered several alien bodies from
   the wreckage of a downed UFO. These bodies
   were taken to an above-top-secret section in the
   facility reserved for only the most senior of government officials. Autopsies have been performed on
   the beings, including the small alien I am looking
   at right now. The only problem is, this alien was
   alive when they started the autopsy. The government is not only covering up the existence of aliens
   but they actually tortured this poor creature and
   opened him up while he was still alive. I'm making
   this recording in case something happens to
   me— Hey, give me that. No, I didn't see anything.
   No, I swear. Hey, wait, stop, don't do that! Leave
   me alone! I don't want to die! Noooooo!

DR. QUINONES: Mr. Williams, wake up, wake up,
   come out of it!

MR. WILLIAMS: What, what, where am I?

DR. QUINONES: You're okay, no one's going to harm
   you.

MR. WILLIAMS: What happened?

DR. QUINONES: Nothing happened. We were just talking. You can relax.

MR. WILLIAMS: Okay.

WILMORE: Doctor, can I talk to you for a moment?

This is the end of the tape. I asked the doctor his personal opinion and he felt Mr. Williams had recounted a genuine experience. I wasn't so sure. Although it was very compelling and dramatic, and as far as I know there was no Area 51 movie or TV show, I was still skeptical. The FOX network did show an alien autopsy special and who knows? Maybe he was channeling watching that show along with something else. I suppose I'll never know. One thing is for sure though, if a brotha has had an actual close encounter of the black kind, it probably happened a long time ago, in a galaxy far, far away.

If Not an Apology,
at Least a "My Bad"

*W*ilmore always believed in the power of words. In the following piece, he tries to help a would-be contrite America find the proper ones.

America has always had a strained relationship with its black citizens. No one can deny that most of it stems from slavery. Some black leaders have argued that before the country can even begin to heal from these terrible wounds, a federal apology is needed. So far that hasn't come. Some individual states have issued apologies in an effort to wipe clean the dirty akashic record, but many feel even these efforts have fallen short.

For example, the New Jersey apology was "the vestiges of slavery are ever before African-American citizens, from the overt racism of hate groups to the subtle racism encountered when requesting health care, transacting business, buying a home, seeking quality public education and college admission, and enduring pretextual traffic stops and other indignities." The response from the black community was a collective "what the fuck was that?"

The problem, from the black perspective, is not the intent behind the apology but the apology itself. It doesn't sound like anything. It was as impersonal as someone taking your order at the drive-thru at a Carl's Jr. The only thing missing was "Do you want fries with that?" And ironically, blacks do want fries with that. Especially if it's a shake. In other words, we want an apology that will satisfy us like a trip to McDonald's. And if you've seen any McDonald's commercial with brothas dancing around, you know how much we love Mickey D's.

The problem from the federal government's point of view is more complicated. How do they issue an apology for something that happened so long ago? Anybody who was a slave is dead, as is anyone who was a slave owner. Americans today feel that since they had nothing to do with it, why should they feel sorry? Also, millions of Americans are descendants of immigrants who came over after slavery and weren't involved at all. This also holds true for blacks whose grandparents are immigrants and don't share a history of slavery themselves. Where do they fit in the apology?

Personally, I feel the federal government should stop worrying about hurting people's feelings and bite the bullet. It really isn't that hard. In fact, there are many different ways the government can apologize and save face at the same time. I've come up with a few suggestions.

THE "MY BAD" APOLOGY

This universal show of contrition works really well with brothas. It was first developed in pick-up basketball games and then evolved into almost any situation where an apology is needed. It's pretty simple and can be worked into almost any presidential address. For example, the president is giving a speech on, let's say, the economy. Right in the middle of it, he veers off and mentions slavery. He then says, "Oh, and while we're talking about that horrible institution, I'd just like to say to my fellow Americans whose ancestors may have been afflicted, my bad." And you're done. Believe me, every brotha in every barber shop will nod their head and say, "Aw, don't worry about it man." And if the president ends this apology with a double fist pump to the chest, it'll make brothas feel even better.

The "my bad" apology also blows right by white people, which is another added plus. I can't recommend this highly enough.

THE "GUY" APOLOGY

Slavery is a very sensitive issue and I don't have to reiterate how touchy brothas are. So the "guy" apology (where you dance around the subject and let the other person fill in the blanks in their own minds) is a wonderful choice. This is one that the president would do face-to-face with a so-called black leader to get the proper rhythm. It would go something like this:

PRESIDENT: Hey, so-called black leader, about that um, you know, that bullshit that went down, you know, um . . .

SO-CALLED BLACK LEADER: You mean the—

PRESIDENT: Yeah, that. Um, you know, that shit was uh, that shit was not, uh—

SO-CALLED BLACK LEADER: That shit was not right.

PRESIDENT: Exactly. And I just want you to know, that um, you know, I would never, um—

SO-CALLED BLACK LEADER: Man, you don't even have to say it, I feel you.

PRESIDENT: Thanks, so-called black leader, cause I would hate to have something like that, you know, come between us.

SO-CALLED BLACK LEADER: It won't. Now give me some dap.

He gives him some dap (it's like a high five but it's not) and he's done. This apology, if done well, can let everybody off the hook without all the messy emotional stuff.

THE "ABSENT-MINDED" APOLOGY

This apology is a very sneaky though effective tactic, because it allows the government to apologize for slavery while pretending as if it already has. This also has the advantage of seeming spontaneous, which gives it a very organic feel.

For instance, the president is taking questions from the press corps and someone says, "When is the United States government going to apologize for slavery?" The president merely feigns surprise and says, "We haven't apologized for slavery? Wow, I thought that was done a long time ago." I guarantee you this will throw people off their game. Immediately they'll come back with, "Hell no, you haven't apologized for slavery!" The president stays with the ruse and says, "I could've sworn one of the last two presidents apologized already. You know what, let me check into that but in the meantime I agree with you."

Do you see what I did there? By adopting a sympathetic attitude coupled with a puzzled recollection and then topped off with agreeing with them, he is able to squash discussion without alienating either side. And on top of that, he never really even apologizes! Bravo.

THE "BURY THE LEAD" APOLOGY

This is also a sneaky apology but is accomplished through misdirection instead of misrecalling. The basic idea is to bury the apology inside of a speech with a very distracting topic.

For instance, the president could be giving a speech to announce the first brothas who will be sent to Mars. Right before the most interesting part, apologize for slavery and then continue. Everyone will be so interested and caught up in the brothas going to Mars announcement that no one will pay much attention to the apology. Nonetheless, you've said you're sorry and can move on. And if anyone ever challenges you, tell them to check the transcripts of your speech.

Word of caution, this should be done only on a Friday so it will be guaranteed to be buried in the press the next day.

Side note: It would be awesome if brothas got to go to Mars!

THE "IRRESPONSIBLE CELEBRITY" APOLOGY

This is the rambling type of apology where you seem very sincere and contrite but you never quite admit to anything and almost blame any bad feelings on the other person. And since this is primarily a narcissistic apology, you don't have to worry about promising reparations when you're done. Just pledge to go to rehab or counseling and all's good. It works something like this: "If anybody was offended or took the institution of slavery in the wrong way, the United States deeply regrets that it happened. I am immediately instituting sensitivity classes for all government employees and their families so the healing process can begin. Once again, I can't tell you how ashamed this government feels in regards to possibly having some citizens misinterpret or misconstrue our historical behavior, which we regret, in the wrong way."

Tip: In order to really pull this off, be sure to wear an extremely sad and contrite face with your eyes looking down the entire time. You can't miss.

THE "SHAKING YOUR TURKEY NECK" APOLOGY

This works only if you have enough fat under your chin to constitute a turkey neck. It was first popularized in the films of the 1930s and was more a show of indignation than an apology. A pudgy patron of society would suffer an indignity and cry out, "This is unmitigated gall! Unmitigated gall, I tell you!" Because this is so old school and no one says "unmitigated gall" anymore, this probably shouldn't be the "go to" apology. But in a pinch, I like it for its boldness. There is no better show of solidarity for a cause than when the apologizer is more outraged than the apologizee.

Here's how it might play: when discussing the notion of an appropriate apology for slavery, the president or government official shakes his turkey neck on the words "inexcusable, unconscionable, and deplorable."

For example, "This country's actions were INEXCUSABLE, UNCONSCIONABLE, and represented the most DEPLORABLE of deeds, I tell you! The most DEPLORABLE of deeds!"

Don't be afraid of this technique. Brothas will be so impressed by your anger that they'll probably overlook the fact that you didn't really apologize.

THE "YOU GO FIRST" APOLOGY

I love this particular approach because it really requires an enormous set of balls. The idea is to get the black community to apologize for something first and then you piggyback the slavery apology on top of that. I know, it sounds unlikely, but with the perfect blend of timing and panache this could be quite effective. The downside is you could be waiting forever for black people to apologize for something. Don't let that stop you though, because as each day passes there are more and more things that blacks may feel deserve contrition on their part.

For example, O.J. Simpson. The longer he's out of jail and playing golf, the more black people may feel they need to apologize for making him the face of their oppression.

The apology might go like this:

SO-CALLED BLACK LEADER: You know what, this O.J. thing has gotten completely out of hand. We are so sorry we backed this loser in the first place. We just want to say—

GOVERNMENT OFFICIAL: (interrupting) You don't even have to go on. I completely know what you're talking about. Just like we hate what happened with that whole slavery thing. We totally feel your pain.

Even though it sounds a bit colloquial, "totally feeling" black people's pain goes a long way in the community. Good luck.

THE "TEARFUL JIMMY SWAGGART" APOLOGY

This is probably the most dramatic of apologies and requires a president or government official with a very large emotional reservoir. You literally have to cry your eyes out in anguished sorrow. And you must not—I repeat, must not—fake it. A good sorrowful phrase is "We have sinned! Please forgive us Lord, we have sinnnnnnnned!" The more blubber and snot you can muster during this over-the-top show of regret the better.

Though this is an actual apology, it takes reparations off the table because everyone will feel so bad for you.

THE "MY OPPRESSION IS WORSE THAN YOUR OPPRESSION" APOLOGY

This is a tough one because there aren't too many grievances worse than slavery. The closest is sexism. Women have been treated poorly pretty much since the beginning of time. Brothas had a good run during the Egyptian period and a few flashes in the Middle Ages.

You need a high-ranking female government official (of course, a female president is ideal) to face the press. She should make it clear, through the use of hand gestures, eye rolling, and impatient exhaling that slavery is nothing compared to what women have faced. A great technique is to mutter something under her breath that is impossible to make out except for the words "women" and "had it worse."

This is most useful when you want to keep brothas from holding on to the moral high ground. Because we all know, as long as brothas have the moral high ground, they will throw it back in your face.

THE "THROW IT IN WITH ALL THE OTHER APOLOGIES" APOLOGY

You don't even have to make a big deal about it with this apology. Just start apologizing for everything. Somewhere in the middle of your rant, just throw in, "Oh and slavery, too." This sounds a little callous, but trust me, if you are apologizing for some serious enough shit, no one will notice.

I hope these suggestions help our government to do the right thing when it comes to healing the rift that has been a part of this country for way too long. And don't get too caught up on which one to use, because at the end of the day, no matter what you say, black people won't believe it. Nevertheless, we still want to hear you say it anyway. Sorry.

It's Okay to Hate Black People
Who Work at McDonald's at the Airport
(It Doesn't Make You Racist)

*M*any of you are familiar with Mr. Wilmore's *controversial book on race* Why Black People Are Funny (Strange and Ha Ha) *published a few years ago. This was very popular on college campuses and prison libraries. What many of you didn't know was there was a chapter missing, a chapter Wilmore wanted included but was prevented from doing so by his publisher. This, finally, is that controversial missing chapter.*

Hate is not racism. Though racists certainly do hate, haters aren't necessarily racists. There are safe levels of hate and unsafe levels of hate. For instance, it is not right to hate people based on skin color, ethnicity, religion, or sexual orientation. Those are unsafe levels of hate. On the other hand, hating people on the basis of where they work is perfectly acceptable. In many cases, it can be cathartic, exhilarating, and just downright fun. Very safe levels of hate.

Let me give you an example. I hate black people who work at McDonald's at the airport. I'm not kidding, I really do. "But Larry, they're black." I know. "You can't hate them." Yes, I can, because they hate me. They hate you too, by the way.

Think about it. They work at McDonald's at the airport. Come on, you would hate you too. "They hate me because they work at McDonald's?" At the airport. That's the important part, the airport. "Baggage handlers work at the airport, do they hate you too?"

No, they handle your bags, which means they get to go through your shit and take what they want. They probably don't like you but they certainly don't hate you. "Can you prove this?" Of course. Why else would I have a hypothetical person ask hypothetical questions?

I visited several McDonald's at various airports and secretly recorded the encounters. I then discussed these encounters with noted Russian behaviorist Dr. Dimitri Domachowska. The following is the transcript of that meeting.

WILMORE: Thank you for coming, Doctor. I really appreciate it. Sorry for the mixup at the hotel.

DIMITRI: Quite all right. My clothes should be completely dry by this evening.

WILMORE: Good, good. I want you to listen carefully to this recording. Don't make up your mind too quickly. Just keep an open mind and we'll discuss it on the other side. Okay?

DIMITRI: Yes.

WILMORE: Great, okay, here we go.

I start the playback of the recording as the doctor leans back and listens intently.

Playback

WILMORE: (whispering) This is Larry Wilmore in line at McDonald's at Kennedy Airport in New York. I have a hypothesis and I am here to see if there's any validity to it. I'm prepared to be proven wrong, but from the looks of the sourpuss that's behind the counter up ahead, I don't think it's going to be even close. There seems to be a lot of unease from the customers who are waiting for their food. It doesn't look like pangs of hunger as much as a collective agitation. As if they've all been dissed in a manner that has stripped off a bit of their humanity. I may talk to them in a bit but first let me place my order and see if my suspicions are valid.

We hear the voice of the counter person. She's barely audible and speaks in the most detached "I could give a shit" voice you can imagine.

COUNTER PERSON: Next.

WILMORE: Uh, yes, I'd like the number three, please.

COUNTER PERSON: Meedlah?

WILMORE: I'm sorry?

COUNTER PERSON: (overenunciating) Medium or large?

WILMORE: Um, can I have small?

COUNTER PERSON: We don't have small, just medium or large.

WILMORE: That doesn't make any sense. I mean, wouldn't the medium technically be the small? Or the large, medium?

COUNTER PERSON: Apply for cook and see?

WILMORE: Apply for cook and see? Why would I want to be a—

COUNTER PERSON: (very agitated) Apple pie or cookies?

WILMORE: Uh, no, just the number three. Did we decide on medium or large?

COUNTER PERSON: You said medium.

WILMORE: I didn't say I wanted medium, I was just making a point about the relative use of the term "medium."

COUNTER PERSON: (ignoring) That'll be six twenty-six.

WILMORE: I guess medium's okay.

COUNTER PERSON: Out of twenty.

WILMORE: Thank you. Do I pick up my food over there?

COUNTER PERSON: Next.

I stopped the playback. I then turned to the doctor.

WILMORE: Impressions?

DIMITRI: This seems like a very typical exchange one might have at a fast-food restaurant. Nothing extraordinary.

WILMORE: Nothing extraordinary? You didn't hear the hate?

DIMITRI: I don't think I would characterize her tone as hate. Perhaps some latent passive aggressiveness but certainly not hatred.

WILMORE: What do you call barely speaking over a whisper so I have to strain to hear every word she said?

DIMITRI: You could call it rude or poor customer service but I still think it's a stretch to characterize it as hatred.

WILMORE: Would you change your mind if I told you she was black?

DIMITRI: I don't understand what that has to do
  with anything.

WILMORE: You don't have to worry about being
  politically correct, Doctor. I can take it.

DIMITRI: I don't understand what you are saying.
  What does black have to do with how a person feels?

WILMORE: Seriously, Doctor, you won't offend me. I'm
  not proud of the fact that black people who work at
  McDonald's at the airport hate us. As a person of
  color, it does not give me cause for celebration.

DIMITRI: Perhaps you are projecting this feeling out of
  a sense of frustration with poor service.

WILMORE: Do you know what a playa hater is, Doctor?

DIMITRI: I'm sorry, what was that?

WILMORE: Playa hater.

DIMITRI: I don't know this term. Is it Jung?

WILMORE: A playa hater is someone who hates a
  "playa" because that "playa" has "game" that the

"hater" doesn't. Instead of hating the "game," he hates the "playa." That's why you always hear people say, "Don't hate the playa, hate the game."

DIMITRI: I have not heard such a thing. In Russia we don't have playas.

WILMORE: You do. They just haven't had game long enough for anyone to seriously hate.

DIMITRI: I'm not sure if I am following. Sorry.

WILMORE: That's all right. Let me break it down. I did not have any "game" going on while at McDonald's. I wasn't dressed flashy, no tattoos, wasn't with a white girl, I was chill. With me?

DIMITRI: I think.

WILMORE: She was throwing me all that hate with no game on my side. In other words, she was not hating the playa or the game, she was just hating. Now do you follow?

DIMITRI: Do you have any scientific evidence for what you are espousing?

WILMORE: Well, I'm not a scientist but I do have evidence. I also went to a coffee shop at the same airport and secretly taped the encounter. Keep in mind, these are black people that work at the airport. The difference is they work at Starbucks. I think you'll be surprised at what I found.

I played back the recording for the doctor.

WILMORE: (whispering) Wow. I've already noticed quite a difference in the air just standing here in line. The level of agitation is decidedly lower. There's some but not at the levels I found at Mickey D's.

COUNTER PERSON: May I help you?

WILMORE: (still whispering) Nice. "May I help you" instead of the hateful "Next." (To the counter person) Yes, I'd like a small coffee.

COUNTER PERSON: The tall?

WILMORE: Um, yeah, if that's the small. I don't know why it's so hard to call something small these days.

COUNTER PERSON: That'll be one sixty-two, please.
Actually we used to have a "short" as our "small"
and the "tall" was the "tall." But after a while,
no one wanted the "short," so now the "tall"
is the "small." It's koo koo but people don't care.
Here's your change and here's your tall. Have a
nice day.

WILMORE: Thank you. You have a nice day too.

I stop the recording and confront the doctor once again.

WILMORE: Okay Doctor, you tell me, what the fuck
was that?

DIMITRI: It sounded like another typical exchange.
This time, I would say, the sales person was much
more polite.

WILMORE: Mmm-hmm. So you agree with me that
she did not hate me?

DIMITRI: I did not detect anything like hate, so, yes,
I suppose I would agree.

WILMORE: Great. Now why do you think black people
who work at McDonald's hate us?

DIMITRI: I'm sorry, but I have to disagree with your hypothesis.

WILMORE: But you do agree with me that it's okay to hate them because they hate us?

DIMITRI: No, I don't know why you insist on wanting to hate people—

WILMORE: Black people.

DIMITRI: Especially your own—

WILMORE: Who work at McDonald's.

DIMITRI: It doesn't matter what they—

WILMORE: At the airport.

DIMITRI: (erupting) Why do you insist on this line of reasoning when it is clear you are the one who is promoting the hate?!

The doctor was obviously very upset, no doubt rankled by the shocking behavior of the black people who work at McDonald's at the airport he'd heard on the tape.

I decided to give him another example.

WILMORE: Take a deep breath and listen very carefully.

Once again, I played him a section of the recording.

WILMORE: Um, I'd like some ketchup, please.

There is no response.

WILMORE: Excuse me, can I have some ketchup, please?

Still there is no response.

WILMORE: Ma'am, I'd just like some ketchup, please.

COUNTER PERSON: (harshly) Here.

WILMORE: Uh, you gave me like, fifteen. I only needed a few.

COUNTER PERSON: Next!

I stopped the recording and turned to the doctor.

WILMORE: Fifteen ketchups. Fifteen, Doctor! One would've been rude. Five would've been snippy but fifteen? God, I hate her!

DIMITRI: Maybe the problem is you. You're drawing an impossible conclusion from such a simple example.

WILMORE: But it's true, Doctor, it's true. She hates me and I hate her and I feel good about it. It's healthy. It's energizing. It's healing if you will.

DIMITRI: Hatred is healing?

WILMORE: Absolutely. Racial hatred has been one of the most divisive and destructive issues since the founding of our country. To this day, the legacy of all that hatred is manifested in harmful ways that we'll be trying to fix for years to come. Whites in particular bear a tremendous amount of guilt for the sins of their forefathers. Sins they themselves would not even fathom committing but they bear the guilty scars anyway. Could you imagine how healing it would be for white people, who've accepted they can't hate black people, to be able to hate black people who work at McDonald's at the airport? It would be huge! Now, I'm not advocating violence. I'm merely looking for a way for pent-up bad feelings and misplaced bias to find a healthy outlet. And if you're black you get to hate your own. How fucking awesome is that?

DIMITRI: I think you are a hate monger.

WILMORE: Yes. But I'm mongering healthy hate. Come on. Think about a group that you're not supposed to hate. Imagine them working at McDonald's at the airport and you'll understand what I'm saying.

DIMITRI: I suppose if Lithuanians worked at McDonald's at the airport, it would feel good to hate them.

WILMORE: Exactly. Thank you, Doctor.

As I said to the doctor, my point is not to promote hatred but to release it. Hatred in the wrong hands can be a tool of destruction. But directed at the proper targets, it can be an instrument of redemption. I look forward to the day when we can hate all of God's people who work at McDonald's at the airport. But for now, I'll take black people who work at McDonald's at the airport. I really hate them.

The End of Racism

In one of Wilmore's more controversial pieces, he contemplates a world without racism.

I hate racism. It's one of the worst scourges to ever afflict mankind. So many awful things in the world would've never existed but for racism. If it was responsible only for slavery and nothing else, it would still be hard to beat. Pound for pound, racism is hands-down the worst of all the "isms." If this is all true, don't we want it to stop? Don't we want to see the end of racism? It ain't necessarily so.

I know this may sound heretical to some but when it comes to racism, I'm overly cautious. I just know that racism is sneaky. Personally, even if it did end I would never believe it. Like a persistent cold sore, racism can rear its ugly head at the most inopportune situations.

Plus, it takes time. We didn't get this racist overnight. It's like losing weight. It took thousands of years to put all that hatred on our thighs. You can't just go on an Oprah "fat in the wagon" crash diet and expect it to melt away. John Lennon knew how hard it was. He changed "Imagine no racism" to "Imagine no possessions" because even he couldn't imagine no racism.

No, we have to acknowledge that it's here to stay, at least for the time being. And we better learn to accept it and move on. To be honest with you, I'm not even sure if I want it to go. Whoa, whoa, whoa, Larry, what the f? Racism is bad. Yeah, but so is putting people out of work. What's going to happen to Al Sharpton, Jesse Jackson, and all the other angry preachers if racism goes away? I'll tell you what's going to happen. They'll be in the unemployment line. Do you know how humiliating that would be for men of their stature to have to hear some overworked government employee ask them, "Did you find any racism today? Did you look for any racism today?" That is not right.

People always say "race relations have come a long way but let's acknowledge they still need to go further." Why? What if we've peaked? What if this is as far as we really should go? Don't we need some tension and conflict to keep life interesting? I, for one, can say that interracial sex would not be nearly as exciting if it weren't for racism. In fact, that's the whole point!

I propose that as ugly as racism is (and it's real ugly), maybe it needs to stick around for a while. Unfortunately it's part of our family. And if you had an ugly member of your family, you wouldn't be clamoring for ways to get rid of him or her. You'd try to get along the best you could. Okay Larry, now you've gone too far. Hear me out. I think I've got a handle on this.

First of all, not everything that seems racist is racist. The problem is that people are so touchy these days everything gets that label just to avoid conflict. Though what ends up happening is more conflict is created by falsely labeling a nonracist incident. Well, if it sounds racist and feels racist but it's not racist, what is it? There's a better term. It might just not be "brotha friendly."

"Brotha friendly" is a term that needs to be in our daily racial jargon. It doesn't replace "racist" or "bigot" but provides a soft landing area for situations that don't call for such harsh accusation. It's the penumbra for intolerance, if you will. The penumbra is the space between shadow and light. "Brotha friendly" can be the penumbra between ignorance and enlightenment.

For example, it would be easy for a young brotha in South Central Los Angeles to label a Korean grocer racist because she won't take her eyes off him while he's shopping. But what if she's not racist? What if she got hornswaggled by another brotha who was shoplifting a few days earlier and is just a tad leery? She doesn't think blacks are inferior, she's just not very brotha friendly.

So "brotha friendly" is a term we should embrace to slowly wean us off the word "racist" and get used to the idea of naked intolerance. In other words, we must look forward to the day when we can hate someone not for the color of their skin but for the content of their character. If we are to reach this utopia, we've got a lot of work to do.

First of all, we need some sort of campaign to educate the public on "brotha friendly" as soon as possible. The more people are able to understand and use this distinction, the easier things get. Here're a few examples to get us started.

REDNECKS: Used to be racist. Now just not brotha friendly.

WHITE TRASH: Used to be not brotha friendly. Now, by and large, brotha friendly.

THE GOVERNMENT: Used to be racist and not brotha friendly. Now, somewhat racist but also somewhat brotha friendly.

COUNTRY MUSIC: Racist but brotha friendly.

COUNTRY SINGERS: Not racist but not brotha friendly.

THE SIMPSONS: Not racist but not very brotha friendly.

FAMILY GUY: Racist but very brotha friendly.

MENTHOL CIGARETTES: Racist but unfortunately very brotha friendly.

DEMOCRATS: Used to be racist and not brotha friendly. They're still racist but very brotha friendly.

REPUBLICANS: Used to be very racist but brotha friendly (party of Lincoln). Now just a tad racist but not very brotha friendly.

BASKETBALL: Not racist and very brotha friendly.

HOCKEY: Not racist but not very brotha friendly.

GOLF: Racist but getting more brotha friendly (Tiger).

GOLF COUNTRY CLUBS: Racist and not brotha friendly.

SUSHI: Not racist but not brotha friendly.

WATERMELON AND FRIED CHICKEN: Very racist but extremely brotha friendly.

These are just a few examples to get us jump-started. Once we have a better understanding of the issues that divide us, we can divide over us and not the issues.

But it's not going to be easy. For one thing, brothas tend to see racism in just about everything. I knew a brotha who tried to convince me that hurricanes were racist. I'm serious. He said, "They gather off the coast of Africa, then head across the ocean till they reach the deep South. What does that remind you of?" He then added, "And why are there no hurricanes with black names? What does that tell you?"

I have to admit, he had a point. Hurricanes do seem pretty racist. And the only ones with even remotely black names were Wanda and Bertha. I looked it up.

Maybe I'm deluding myself. Maybe racism is so strong and virulent that the only solution is to call it out even when we're wrong in an effort to destroy it completely. And if we can do that, we can really achieve a truly utopian world.

Of course, utopia comes from the Greek words "ou," which means not or no, and "topos," which means place. In other words, utopia literally means "no place."

Utopia may not be racist but it sure doesn't sound very brotha friendly.